Democracy
in the Administration
of Higher Education

Democracy
in the Administration
of Higher Education

EDITED BY HAROLD BENJAMIN

Essay Index Reprint Series

BOOKS FOR LIBRARIES PRESS
FREEPORT, NEW YORK

Originally published as Tenth Yearbook of the
John Dewey Society.

Copyright 1950 by Harper & Brothers.

Reprinted 1972 by arrangement with
Harper & Row, Publishers, Inc.

Library of Congress Cataloging in Publication Data

Benjamin, Harold Raymond Wayne, 1893-1969, ed.
    Democracy in the administration of higher education.

    (Essay index reprint series)
    Original ed. issued as the tenth Yearbook of the
John Dewey Society.
    1. Universities and colleges--Administration--
Addresses, essays, lectures. I. Title. II. Series:
John Dewey Society. Yearbook, 10th.
LB2341.B45 1972   378.1'008   72-3344
ISBN 0-8369-2892-X

PRINTED IN THE UNITED STATES OF AMERICA

CONTENTS

v

PART THREE. THE RESPONSIBILITY OF ADMIN-ISTRATION

PREFACE

THE twelve authors of this volume are administrators and teachers whose jobs require constant concern with problems of organizing and administering higher educational institutions. Half of them are professors who carry heavy loads of executive responsibility in addition to instructional service and research tasks. The remainder are university deans or college presidents. All of them work daily at jobs demanding feet-on-the-ground and down-to-earth decisions. They have to be practical in order to get these jobs done acceptably.

In scrutinizing democracy in the administration of higher education, the authors have therefore looked first for practical ways by which the work of higher education might better be done. They have sought those practices in administration which would enable them to transmit their institutions "not only not less but greater and better" than transmitted to them. They have felt that the first claim of their people upon them in their every-day work is that they shall do that work with as good results as possible. They believe that democratic ways are the most practical ways of educating a people. They hold that free men educate themselves most effectively in a condition of self-controlled freedom. They maintain that this freedom is the heart of the existence of a democratic college or university. They regard democratic administration as an instrument for achieving such freedom.

The authors are also theorists. They know that the most truly practical processes in education, as in the other great affairs of life, are those which are most firmly based on sound and adequate theories of action. They believe that the most useful theories are erected upon the strongest and most extensive foundations of practice. They regard the mere practitioner, the simple mechanic of management routines who is proud of his lack of theoretical concepts, as being hopelessly impractical. They look upon the mere dreamer of grand notions, the visionary wrapped wholly in his visions who is contemptuous of the details of administrative practice, as being a dreamer and nothing more. They insist that his claim to represent theory is spurious.

The achievement of mutual support between the theory and the practice of educational democracy requires the discovery and utilization of certain formal, basic relationships among all those engaged in college and university work. The essence of all those relationships is *fairness,* the spirit by which men develop and use the instruments of democracy.

Without this spirit, the most elaborate complex of faculty committees and student conferences, or the most comprehensive machinery of discussion and balloting, will remain crystallized in sterile autocracy. A majority of the total faculty, minus one, can be and sometimes is as dictatorial to that minority of one as any single academic tyrant has ever been. With this spirit, the simplest and most direct measures of communication and action can be the soul of democracy. The letter of university democracy sometimes killeth when the spirit of fairness maketh not alive.

Theory illumines purposes, practice achieves purposes, and *fairness* guards and develops those purposes for every individual. This is a clear-cut and simply stated program for the administration of higher education.

The authors recognize that this program is easier to describe than to carry out in these clear-cut and simple terms. They have therefore attempted in this volume to examine some current practices in the administration of higher educational institutions, to consider whether those practices are soundly based on democratic principles of higher education, and to suggest the consequent responsibilities of administration in making the practices work.

Part One attempts to furnish a theoretical framework. It sketches the purposes of higher education, the principles of democratic association, the character and task of democratic administration, and the story of the college administrator's search for the meaning of his job.

Part Two reviews critically the main practices of administration in determining purposes of higher education, in arranging and carrying on instructional and research activities, in organizing the faculty, in administering policies affecting students and teachers, and in developing democratically effective relationships between governing boards and the institutions.

Part Three combines practice and theory with discussions of how to select and appraise teachers and administrators, how to secure and distribute financial support, how to determine the purposes of the institution, how to study learners on the higher educational level and communities in which and for which they learn, and how to evaluate the program.

The editor expresses his personal appreciation to the members of the Tenth Yearbook Committee and to present and past members of the Executive Board of the Society for their counsel in planning this volume. He is much indebted to Harold B. Alberty of the Ohio State University, Harvey H. Davis of the State University of Iowa, Claude Eggertsen of the University of Michigan, Harold C. Hand of the University of Illinois, Laurence D. Haskew of the University of Texas, H. Gordon Hullfish of the Ohio State University, Charles S. Johnson of Fisk University, Edward J. Sparling of Roosevelt College, and Harold Taylor of Sarah Lawrence College for their hearty cooperation in the authorship of the volume. To his colleagues at the University of

Maryland, R. Lee Hornbake and Gladys A. Wiggin, he is particularly indebted, not only for their contributions as authors but
also for their generous and able assistance in editorial labors. He
acknowledges with warm regard, furthermore, the wise and able
counsel of John B. Schwertman of Roosevelt College in planning
the *Yearbook*.

To the degree that all this cooperation produced an effective
statement, it was a democratic effort. The judgment of its worth
on the counts of both democracy and effectiveness is left to the
John Dewey Society, to that larger fraternity of the authors'
fellow teachers and administrators in the colleges and universities,
and to that greatest society of men everywhere who would be
truly free in their highest education as in their humblest tasks.

                                            HAROLD BENJAMIN

PART ONE
Principles in the Administration of Higher Education

CHAPTER I

THE ROLE OF HIGHER EDUCATION IN AMERICAN DEMOCRACY

HAROLD BENJAMIN
University of Maryland

ADMINISTRATION of any institution, however simple and direct its procedures, is a mere manipulation of red tape whenever it lacks a clear concept of the institution's purposes. In judging the worth of administrative practices in American higher education, therefore, it is first necessary to ask, "What are we trying to do for our people with these colleges and universities?"

WHAT DO AMERICANS WANT HIGHER EDUCATION TO DO?

There are many current answers to this question. One kind of answer, given in a variety of disguises, holds that "higher" education is a matter of training the minds of young people of "higher" capacity, giving them the "higher" truths, and fitting them for the "higher" callings. Formulations of this answer run all the way from cultivation-of-the-intellect-by-universal-knowledge to higher-education-for-higher-character.

Another class of answers to the question of why the colleges should teach is commonly given in descriptions of what they should teach. Lists of "areas" of knowledge, as those of human relationships, the nature of the physical universe, masterpieces of literature, and great musical compositions, are often constructed and formally christened *purposes, objectives,* or *foundations* of the higher wisdom.

Sometimes the area approach to this question is varied by substituting a list of abilities, as critical insight, creative imagination, balanced judgment, skill in using books, integrity, courage, good manners, tolerance, industry, and capacity to write good English.

In a democracy such *ex cathedra* formulations often have little meaning. A democracy is a manner of association whereby men order their own ways for their own benefit. A democratic education is that phase of their association whereby they change their own ways in the direction of their own ideals. The purposes of higher education in a democracy can therefore be discovered only by observing the democracy in action.

Do these people of the United States act as though they want more and better housing, health services, and education in the changed ways of life they envision for themselves? If so, it is the sheerest nonsense to say that the purpose of their universities is exclusively a knowledge-truth, presumably everywhere the same, yesterday, today, and forever, and not the vocational purposes served by colleges for architects, engineers, physicians, and teachers. Do the Americans operate their enterprises in such fashion as to need farmers, merchants, F.B.I. men, and housewives with systematic, full-time education above the age of eighteen or twenty? If they do, they will educate such people in "higher" educational institutions for exactly those purposes. The history of education in the United States is replete with examples of loud and authoritative pronouncements about what should not and could not be done educationally, only to have the people go about doing the "impossible" at once. Tax-supported elementary schools, secondary education for more than ten per cent of the "upper" classes, publicly supported universities, and free junior colleges were all once impossible. Indeed they were commonly so described by some of the highest authorities after they were well on their way to realization.

The purposes of the State University of Osceola or of Dead Coon Lake College are precisely what the people of Osceola or of the Dead Coon Lake country want them to be. Does this mean that the teachers and administrators of these institutions need to be only opinion-pollsters to discover those purposes? Decidedly not. They must study their people with great concern and skill but they must also do much more. They must inform their people on the nature of higher educational instruments which are adequate to the people's purposes. They must inspire their people to formulate and support those purposes. Finally, since they are themselves members of the democratic community, they have the right and the obligation to express themselves in word and action on this as on any other question confronting the democratic community.

How Well Does American Higher Education Study Its Purposes?

The American colleges and universities do not generally carry on this phase of their task very effectively. They avoid it in part perhaps because they do not see it and in even larger part because when they do see it they are afraid of it. It is a difficult task. It can be dangerous. It is almost sure to be dangerous when it is well done. It is much easier to be busy with less important matters that are easy and safe.

Consider, as an example of this concern with the fringes of purpose, the complex of synthetic tradition, shabby-genteel ceremonial, and *ersatz* history which has been constructed around much of the higher education in this country. On some campuses the major share of what passes for intellectual vigor in administrative and faculty circles is devoted to any peripheral activity so long as it carries an aura of scholastic respectability. ·Hence comes the weight given to convocation ceremonies, commencement processions, academic regalia, and claims to institutional antiquity in which one decade or century, however somnolent and decadent, counts for as much as any other. Hence, to some extent, the university senate's lengthy debates on terminology, classification of disciplines, and adjudication of boundary disputes among divisions and departments. Hence, in large part, the nostalgic academic yearning after past glories that often never existed.

It is this yearning, with the timid escapism accompanying it, which has been largely responsible for the ancient fallacy that the modern university is an old institution tied to its colorful and powerful medieval forerunners in many significant ways.

How Did the Medieval University Determine What to Do?

The medieval university, as a matter of fact, bears a relatively slight relationship to modern higher educational institutions. It had no great concern with peripheral matters. It was a lusty institution which well knew what it was trying to do. It set out to perform its tasks in a direct and realistic way. Its color, pomp, ceremonies, customs, and traditions were its own, built from the ground up, or rather from the cobblestones polished by the rough shoes of its brawling, carousing, hungry students. It wore its gowns and tonsures in token of the very practical clerical privileges for which it had to fight. The hood of a master of arts or a doctor of laws was worth good hard cash and sometimes exemption from the gallows. The university broke chancellors who would not heed its wishes and reduced free cities, which dared to draw steel against its masters and students, to the level of mere houskeeping appendages dependent on its favor. It played kings against bishops and even the Papacy against the Empire to carry out what it regarded as its proper functions. It claimed and needed no ancient line of descent. Like the Napoleonic marshal, it could slap itself on the breast and say, "My ancestors? Bah! I am myself an ancestor!"

The medieval university, playing its most distinguished role in the thirteenth and fourteenth centuries, was a democratic institution at a time when Church and State generally avoided even a breath of the notion that anyone other than the pope, the emperor, the king, the bishop, or some similar divinely appointed boss should decide what was best for the people to do and think.

The democracy of the earliest universities arose in response to a need for security in study. Paris was a university of masters because its teachers came from all over Europe. As foreigners in the French capital, they had few rights until they banded themselves together into an association for mutual protection. In Bologna, where the masters were usually citizens of Lombardy, on the other hand, it was the students who were foreigners and who banded themselves together in the *universitas*.

It should be observed here that in the twelfth century the name of the institution itself, that which we now call the University of Paris or the University of Bologna, was *studium generale*. The *universitas* was the association of professors, of students, or of both. The fact that the name of the teaching and student bodies came to be used in place of the name of the institution is in itself a striking piece of evidence of the power and prestige of the *universitas*.

WHY WAS THE EARLY UNIVERSITY STRONG?

The university came into its democracy naturally and forcefully. The *universitas* was a guild, a trade union, of masters as in Paris, or of students as in Bologna. The word *universitas* itself means the *whole*, the *entire group*. In a Paris-type university every member of the association of masters had his vote and voice in every university decision. Every teacher of the arts faculty had as much power as any other teacher in electing the rector, the deans, and the proctor. Every master helped decide when and how the chancellor, representative of the bishop and official granter of licenses to teach, should be opposed, disciplined, or driven from office. If swords or daggers were to be drawn in defense of the university's rights, every master of arts was obligated by his academic oath to be in the fray, leading his students to riot and battle even though the enemy might be the Crown or the Papal Legate. In 1225 Cardinal Romano, official delegate in Paris of the Holy See, was rushed out of town under the protection of royal troops to save him from death at the hands of masters and students. He had seized and broken the University seal, an act which seemed to him entirely warranted by his plenary powers in view of the fact that neither king nor pope had granted the seal. As the battering rams crashed through the front doors of his princely residence, he was probably not thinking of anything much except how to escape through the back door, but he could have mused on the turbulent and scholarly beginnings of a concept of human association which would disturb autocrats for at least seven hundred years more.

The students and masters often used their democratic powers in ways that seem foolish now and were perhaps foolish then. The rector of the University of Paris, for example, was elected for very brief terms, six weeks or less, until 1280 when the masters decided that his term should be long enough to permit him to work out his policies over a considerable period. They lengthened the term to three months. Even with this long term, it was apparent that almost any master could be rector in time, take the oath of allegiance from the bachelors of arts, hold precedence even over cardinals and princes of royal blood, and in his own person represent and speak for that *universitas*, the whole outfit, the whole works, where one scholar was as good as another and could attain brief magnificence only by the will of his fellows.

The medieval university in its period of early strength knew what it was doing. It had little or no notion that its objectives were subjects of study in themselves. It believed that it was training men, scholars, for definite professions. Its arts faculty trained teachers. Its medical, theological, and law faculties were strictly professional schools. A teacher had to acquire materials for instruction and learn the techniques of lecture and disputation for using those materials with students. The physician had to learn what to prescribe for each disease. The lawyer and the theologian similarly had a level of craftsmanship to reach. It was only when the medieval university ceased to be important that ideas of what today might be called "general education" concerned the masters very much.

On the other side of the account, opposed to the two great sources of the university's strength—its democratic organization and its clear-cut goals—there were two great weaknesses which were largely responsible for the decline of higher education from the fourteenth century onward.

The first of these weaknesses was the university's divorcement from the people. It was a state within a state, a community so walled in from outside influences that it could not adequately develop and grow with the general community, local, national, or international. It was so jealous of its democratic fortress of learning that it learned in narrower and narrower descending spirals, until at last it sat regarding its scholastic navel in almost complete mystical uselessness.

The second weakness was closely associated with the first. In its first centuries, the university was eager for new texts, new methods of teaching, new approaches to professional tasks. When even a great professor taught what the students regarded as antiquated materials, he was howled down as an old fogy. But then the notion of timeless culture crept into the universities. Aristotle was studied just because he was Aristotle. Peter of Lombard's *Sentences* came to have more and more authority as they accumulated year after year of professorial moss. At last the university sat mumbling over its great books, while the pioneer makers of the modern world rode outside its gates on quests the university could not comprehend.

How Can American Higher Education Put Its Purposes into Action?

The university today, using the term to include higher education in general, has a greater task before it, a greater role to play, than had its medieval predecessor, precisely because it serves a greater society for greater purposes than did the *studium generale* of Bologna, Salamanca, Paris, Oxford, or Prague. It is in these purposes and the instruments for achieving them that the modern university must find its true meaning, its real color, and its whole *raison d'être*.

The university of the United States at this mid-point of the twentieth century, like the medieval university, has its strengths and it weaknesses for its role. It must examine those strengths and weaknesses with concern and wisdom, for it can be destroyed or it can be raised to the heights of greatness by either its strengths or weaknesses.

The first great strength of the American university lies in its formal, organizational relation to its people. Paris was a trade union of masters and Bologna a guild of students, but the American university is neither. It is a corporation of representatives of the people. This is the greatest single contribution of the United States to the history of higher education. The invention and development of the lay board, representing the citizens of a whole political unit as in the case of municipal and state universities, or representing the people of a religious, cultural, or other grouping which to them appears significant for higher education as in the case of most so-called private universities, have made possible the tremendous growth and vitality of university education in this country.

The weaknesses attendant on this uniquely American system of control are outlined in detail in Chapter IX. Here it is enough to say that they are mainly defects of technique rather than of principle. Bad as many boards of trustees and regents have been in their handling of particular institutions, they have kept the American university close to the people and have thereby given it a basis for democratic effectiveness which no *universitas* strictly of masters or of students could hope to achieve.

The second great strength of the American university lies in its specialization of administrators. Andrew D. White, Charles W. Eliot, William Rainey Harper, David Starr Jordan, and Lotus D. Coffman would hardly have made a ripple in American higher education if they had been rectors elected for only three months, nine months, or even five years. The American university benefited immeasureably by the system which took those men and gave them years of administrative experience to prepare, mature, and execute great policies. The same observation can be made concerning deans and department chairmen.

There is a concomitant weakness, however, with this strength. With the growing specialization and power of administrators, the modern "masters" have given less and less of their attention to policy matters of great moment. This is partly because, like all human beings, they are lazy and avoid whenever possible the labor of thought. "Let the dean do it—he gets paid **for making** decisions." More often, however, it is because the **professional** administrator—the president, the dean, the **department** head—expresses his scorn, either directly and **brutally or** tactfully and hypocritically, of the amateurish efforts **of a young** instructor or assistant professor to concern himself **with** questions of policy which are so far above his inexperienced head.

IS PROFESSIONAL EXPERIENCE A HANDICAP IN COLLEGE ADMINISTRATION?

This is one of the **most dangerous** weaknesses in American higher education today. **It causes** some universities to descend to the level of **believing** that a trained administrator, a man who has run **banks, oil** companies, armies, or political parties is a wonderful **"find"** for a university presidency. Far from being disturbed **by the** new "scholar's" lack of the most elementary **preparation** for academic leadership, even certain faculty members **appear** to think that they are lucky to have someone **uncontaminated** by educational experience; they appear to rate **their own** academic preparation so low as to think that possession **of the** training and degrees of a university teacher tends to **disqualify** a man for high administrative position in the **university.** Perhaps this is because university teachers are **increasingly** kept from "meddling" in administrative matters. **They are** therefore supposed to be innocent of the guile **and commonsense** developed so superbly in county, state, and **national** politics, in the slick maneuverings of the market **place, or** in the weighty process of approving the decisions of a **glittering** military staff.

One feature of this **deterioration** of professional pride and competence in the **central work** of the university is found in the current disdain **for teaching,** a disdain expressed in actions rather than **words. There** is no dean of any school or college in any American **university** who cannot teach at least one course or seminar, if he is competent to hold a deanship, and who would not benefit as an administrator from such teaching, yet in the smallest institutions many "masters" hasten to discard all teaching tasks as soon as the magic mantles of administrative authority settle upon their shoulders. Even department chairmen sometimes appear to measure their administrative worth by the fewness and brevity of their actual contacts with students, while the president who goes into a classroom under any circumstances, even as the most casual lecturer and even when his institution is not as big as a moderate sized high school, is so rare as to be practically nonexistent. The president of a small college usually feels that he is so tied up with grave administrative responsibilities that he can talk only with deans and directors. When he lectures it must be in the big auditorium on the broadest possible subjects—what to do about communism, how to avoid atomic warfare, or some other large topic—for which task he has been prepared by being an administrator.

What Higher Education Needs

Solutions for this weakness, by which specialization has proceeded to the point where already a great gap is widening between teachers and administrators, are suggested in Chapter VIII. It is mentioned here primarily because it constitutes one of the greatest dangers to the effectiveness of the university. The institution may think it lacks money, but this is never its basic want. The people of the United States will give it every dollar it has brains and imagination enough to use for the higher education of a truly great society. It may think it is in great danger from the meddling of regents and trustees in professional questions, but the regents and trustees will never be any more stupid or mischievous than the quality of the university permits and demands. The great evil faced by the university, the great block to its achievement of truly stirring and meaningful purpose for its people, is this possible breakdown in its concept of the roles of its teachers, its students, and its administrators.

Democracy is only an instrument to get things done for a people. It is only a tool for utilizing the maximum intelligence of a group. The university needs democracy not because democracy is a sacred word but because the university has to get something done for its people. If it does not get done what the people need to have done, the people will once again ride by the university as they rode by its medieval predecessor. If the modern American university finally demonstrates that it received from its academic ancestors too many costumes and ceremonials and not enough principles and springs of action it too can end up staring in scholarly solemnity at its institutional navel.

CHAPTER II

THE SOCIAL RESPONSIBILITIES
OF HIGHER EDUCATION

CHARLES S. JOHNSON
Fisk University

T HE social responsibilities of higher education in a democracy are probably more often discussed than actually shouldered. Perhaps the main reasons for this situation are first that they appear to be heavy responsibilities, and second that higher education is not commonly aware of its own strength. Indeed, educational institutions on all levels tend to underestimate their real powers. In a democracy it is particularly necessary that schools and colleges should know definitely what they can do.

What can they do to and for their society?

THE JAPANESE EDUCATIONAL SYSTEM

Recently the author had the opportunity, as a member of a commission sent out under the auspices of the Department of State and the Department of the Army to advise our military government in Japan on desirable changes in the Japanese educational system, to observe the nature and effects of, an educational system very different from our own. An outstanding lesson from this experience was the demonstration of how determinative the educational process can be—that is, how far education can go, when centrally controlled and directed with specific purposes in mind, to mold the ideas, the culture, and the economy of a people. The Japanese educational system was designed to inculcate in the people certain attitudes toward the state and its rulers, certain rules of conduct and concepts of history, which would make them willing and unquestioning servants of a national militaristic purpose. History shows that the system succeeded remarkably well.

The Japanese experience is not an argument for our taking over the content or even the methods of that educational process, but it does suggest to American educators that they may not have begun to realize the possibilities of what education can do. It is primarily a question of determining the goals to be reached and of making sure that every aspect of the educational process is directed toward those goals. It might be objected that this would amount to a kind of regimentation which is repugnant to American ideals. This is not necessarily so. It is not necessary to regiment the content of education if its processes are all directed towards a common end. If the goal is democracy, then it should be obtainable by making sure that every part of the educational process is an experience in democratic living.

To go back for a moment to the Japanese experience, it was possible to observe, along with the successes, the defects of such a system, which only showed themselves clearly when it became necessary for the people to adapt themselves to social and political change. An outstanding defect was the lack of development of the social sciences along with the almost hysterical attempt to develop the physical sciences—as a means, of course, of securing the position of Japan in a world dominated by western technology. This feverish concentration on the physical sciences enabled Japan to make a remarkably rapid transition from a weak and backward feudal island to a great power in a military sense. But it left the people themselves less and less able to cushion the shock of transition, either from feudalism to industrialism, or from victory to defeat. One result has been a great deal of disorganization of Japanese life, especially in the cities.

A closely related weakness of this educational system was the complete control over ideas, which exposed the Japanese people to an utterly unrealistic world. History, for example, became a mere rote learning of myths about the origin and importance of the Japanese people and nation, so that the people were completely unprepared to understand the actual course of events, and defeat became a psychological cataclysm of tremendous proportions.

Some Problems of Our Own System

These apparent weaknesses of the Japanese educational system may help us to observe, and perhaps to counteract, some less obvious weaknesses in our own system. Like the Japanese, if not to the same extent, our system has emphasized the physical rather than the social sciences. We are living in a period of tremendous technological advance, but we have not learned the skills and techniques for adapting these advances to social living so that they will bring about a more satisfying life for the individual and more harmonious relationships between groups and nations. In fact, it is our very technological power that has brought about some of the worst evils of our modern society. Wars, depressions, twisted personalities, broken homes, race riots are some of the symptoms arising from the fact that while technology has made great strides forward, our ability to adjust has lagged behind. The sociologists call this a "cultural lag."

Obvious as the situation is, there is as yet no general recognition of it either in our educational systems or in our national social policies. We have set up an atomic control board which has on it various physical scientists who can advise on the uses and development of atomic power. But the board does not include social scientists who might anticipate or give advice on the changes in the lives of people which such developments may bring about—such as, for instance, changes in hours of work, kinds of skills and abilities required, and, even more fundamentally, changes in habits of living, in the relationships of people to one another, in the character and location of cities and towns, and in international relations.

In a general way we can all recognize that the discovery of atomic power has made some kind of world order a necessity. But no one has proposed spending a fraction of what goes into physical research on the development of techniques to prepare people for intelligent participation in such an order. Only a few of our industries, more sensitive to changes which may affect the profit picture, are turning to the social sciences to help them prepare for the future. Dr. William F. Ogburn, of the University of Chicago's Department of Sociology, has recently completed a study, at the request of the airplane industry, of changes in habits of living which may be expected in the light of an expanding air service.

Faculty members of our colleges and universities have an immediate responsibility to their students and to the community at large to rethink their program in terms of the necessity of social adaptation to changing world conditions. Every student, regardless of his field of specialization, ought to be prepared to understand and participate creatively in a rapidly changing social, economic, and political life. Our colleges, moreover, must cease to think of themselves as merely training centers which are preparing individuals *for* life. They must recognize their role as social institutions which function as a part of life. John Dewey defined education as a process by which society renews and perpetuates itself as a society. If this process is to be effective today, the college must be a part of the community, and the community, the life of the society, must be a part of the college, so that each renews and invigorates the other. The college, moreover, cannot teach one thing and be another. If we are going to teach the values of democracy, we must cease to think of democracy only in terms of certain political, economic, and social rights. It is equally essential to learn to live democratically. This means that the educational process itself must be an experience in democratic participation.

What Is the Purpose of American Higher Education?

Behind the failure of much of our education lies confusion and lack of agreement as to the purpose of education. Why do young people go to college, or why do their parents send them there? It has been said that some fathers send their sons to college because they themselves went to college, and that others send them because they never went to college.

Students of today are interested less in the abstract values of education for education's sake than in the more immediate and intimate problems of acquiring, through the medium of education, a new cultural status. They are interested in laying the foundation for personal and economic security, and in eventually finding psychic and emotional satisfaction on a plane of living to which no stigma of inferiority attaches in living freely in a free world.

Freedom and security are difficult for most persons to obtain. If in the world today we think of freedom and security as goals which we can reach as individuals by virtue of our own competitive efforts, we are doomed from the outset to defeat. America has been a land of individualism. We tend to think of our success, our citizenship, our obligations to society, our morality even, in the terms of the individual. In school and college we think we have succeeded if we get high grades, keep out of trouble, and earn a degree showing that we have completed the required number of hours entitling us to a certain academic or vocational status. In the matter of earning a living we think we have succeeded if we can get and keep a better than average job which gives us either a better than average income or a degree of social prestige. In our personal life we think that if we attend church regularly, are kind to our families and honest in our dealing with others, we have fulfilled the demands of morality and good citizenship.

All these concepts are the heritage of a pioneer period when a man's life achievement could actually be to a large extent the result of his own efforts. But today the greatest single factor in our society is modern industrial technology. Its demands and its necessities have changed and are changing our ways of getting a living, our social institutions, and our family relationships. Technological changes have at the same time increased the demand upon government and removed it further from the individual citizen. The war required still further centralization and governmental control. Even though many of the measures involved were considered temporary, they are bound to have a lasting effect upon American life. Unless new methods can be devised to preserve direct citizen participation in government, what we think of as democracy will become more and more a mere form. And thus we are in danger of finding those rights of citizenship for which we have been striving turn to dust at the very moment we are reaching out to grasp them.

Education, in the face of these changes, has a stupendous task. First, it must help young people to win economic security in this society dominated by technology; second, it must help them to find ways of satisfying the basic psychic needs for a sense of belonging and participation in a society whose institutions are becoming constantly bigger, more remote, and more impersonal; third, the educational institutions must be an active force in the community working towards a society in which these satisfactions are available to all.

In general, academic institutions tend to isolate themselves from the community, perhaps because they had their beginnings in medieval times when only a handful of people could even read. This isolation fostered the sterile scholasticism which we associate with the problem of how many angels could dance on the point of a needle.

Colleges Must Work on Society's Problems

Today, however, there is general literacy, and we live by common symbols which can, or should, bind us together. Whether we like it or not, our academic institutions are a part of the community and should expect to give spark and direction to its life. The issues which are live, vital issues in the society should be those on which education is concentrating its resources and its techniques; and what is taught in school should be taught in relation to its function as a part of the social fabric. It is utterly futile, for example, to learn a skill without a functioning acquaintance with the economic structure into which this skill and its human practitioners are expected to fit. Only through such understanding can we achieve a new dignity of work and a new dignity of personality.

Faculties that will embark on a program of defining and furthering these social adaptations will find their job no easy task. They will discover themselves to be in the midst of what we are prone to call controversial issues: union-management relations, adequate provisions for housing and health, and a host of other burning questions.

There is immense importance in the labor movement, even with its weaknesses and its failures, as a means of lending dignity and meaning to the worker's struggle for existence. It meets him where he is: full of isolation and fear, struggling to save his own life, and making a miserable job of it. It tells him he cannot save even his own life in that way; he must work with thousands and millions of others like himself, singly self-condemned in the effort to save themselves, but irresistible when they unite with others to claim their human heritage. It does not meet him at the economic level; that is where he is. But it can give him, if it can only be true to its task, things that are more precious than bread: solidarity and dignity. It should be a function of education to work with the labor movement to make manifest and to develop this larger function of the labor movement. The mistakes of organized labor are largely those that could be corrected by the wisdom and disciplines of the educational institutions.

Housing is another live issue which academic institutions cannot afford to neglect. We tend to think of housing problems as if they were something apart from us, as if we did not ourselves live in houses. It is always a problem of somebody else, or, if we are actually faced with it as a personal necessity, it is conceived in its narrowest sense as a need for so much physical space. Yet, housing is the physical setting for the all-important family life, the core of the social structure. So lethargic have our institutions been to the importance of the whole complex of housing problems that the National Housing Agency is combing the country for persons who can administer programs in this area which no institution has yet found a way of treating in a curriculum.

Health is not ignored in our educational setup, but is left to specialists when it is very largely a matter of social illiteracy. The failure of education to place these problems in a true perspective is illustrated by the spectacle of some doctors fighting federal health measures as a menace to individualism. Any efforts toward a broad attack on the problem are left to private and public agencies outside the schools.

The whole field of community organization desperately

needs the perspective which educational institutions and truly educated persons could bring to it. Today we pay more attention to streets and highways than to people. It needs to be continuously emphasized that the central problem of planning is the problem of community understanding, and the development of a sense of community wider than the individual and family worlds out of whose uncoordinated drives our present planless cities and towns have grown up. There is a tremendous educational task to be done in the presentation of group relations as a phase of community relations—but so far this task is left to occasional pressures and to the press. Our educational institutions have made little effort, for example, to develop public understanding through an objective investigation and presentation of the relationships between restrictive covenants and property values.

The Dangers of This Program

Admittedly, there are difficulties in putting into practice this view of the function of an educational institution. A program of this kind is new and must be formulated. Our colleges have not provided for it in their courses, nor always in their teaching personnel. The teachers have vested interests and established ways and are not always sincere in dealing with these issues. Many of our colleges have been developed in terms of a technical curriculum, and the new knowledge and function cannot easily be fitted in.

The students of the social sciences point out repeatedly that one of the results of modern technology has been to take away the creative satisfaction which a worker used to derive from his work without so far affording any adequate substitute. The same is true of the citizen, who in the old town meeting used to take direct part in governmental decision, and who was personally acquainted with the representative whom he chose to act for him. Now great concentrations of economic power have practically taken over the real direction of government, while many of us are still struggling for its outward symbols.

Not only are these great concentrations dangerous to liberty, but the nature of the resulting institutions makes self-expression and creative participation difficult for most people.

The very essence of democracy is to provide opportunity for participation; creative participation in the on-going process of society is essential to the general welfare, as well as to the welfare of the individual. The effect of huge institutions on the individual psychology is disastrous. . . . Many feel lost and insecure under such circumstances. Since personal relationships are scarce and unsatisfactory, they lack the sense of belongingness.[1]

This is true of members of minority groups who, by their very position in the society, are made to feel that they do not belong.

An understanding of these factors helps to explain many trends which otherwise appear to us simply as evidence of the natural sinfulness of man. It helps to explain why people drink more than they used to, why there are more divorces than there were formerly, why children are less respectful to their parents, and why Congressmen behave as they do. But we are called upon for more than understanding. Our educational institutions—and that includes the administrators, the teachers, and the students—have the responsibility of seeking the way out, the way in which our social organization can catch up with our technological progress so as to satisfy the basic needs of the individual and give expression to the values of a free society.

[1] "The Curse of Bigness" by George B. De Huszar, in *Conflicts of Power in Modern Culture*, edited by Lyman Bryson, Louis Finkenstein & R. M. MacIver (New York: Harper & Brothers, 1947), p. 333.

CHAPTER III

THE TASK OF COLLEGE ADMINISTRATION

HAROLD TAYLOR

Sarah Lawrence College

DURING the past five years, the college president in America has had the honor of being described, discussed, analyzed, and pitied in the journals and the press on the average of half a dozen times each month. His responsibilities as a thinker, manager, speaker, leader, social critic, and fund-raiser have been noted and appraised. Advice to him has come from businessmen, politicians, faculty members, students, parents, alumni, trustees, and people whom he meets on buses. Naturally enough, Mr. Hutchins has written about him, and with the expected disjunctions, has said he must be either strong and disliked, or weak and tolerated—an office boy or an administrator.

None of the advice from any of these sources has been of any use at all to the college president himself. It has simply pointed to the fact that a great deal is expected of him, that a great many people are watching him, and that education in America is important, both in public opinion and in reality.

What Kind of Administrator Is Needed?

One trend, however, can be noted. The administration of colleges and universities has become so complex a problem in finance and personnel that governing officers have sought, in their appointments to the presidency, the services of men with business and administrative records, and, in large measure, have considered intellectual and educational experience as unnecessary to the post. In the twelfth century, at the beginning of the university movement in western civilization, universities were composed of scholars to whom students came to learn, and were administered by the scholars, who elected one of themselves to a yearly or even briefer headship. Occasionally the students themselves administered their own education, to the point of employing their own faculty and moving their own premises.

In America, we have now reached the opposite position. Groups of businessmen, industrial executives, and political appointees of the state, incorporated by charter to control education, now employ presidents to handle the funds to hire a staff of experts to instruct students in the proper professional skills, the intellectual habits and academic folklore of a democratic-capitalist society. Qualities of scholarship, learning, and humanity are not relevant to this task—indeed, in some instances are hindrances. What is needed is sound business sense, good public presence, and a reputation for respectability. In some cases it is desirable in the candidate either to have refused or to have been refused the presidency of the United States.

In fact, so much depends upon the financial success of the university undertaking that it is impossible for a university to advance in its proper work without a continuous and efficient program of money-raising and a series of projects to increase income. This is now the major responsibility of the chief administrative officer, the university president. Our American universities have become huge institutions in which the academic, student, and employee affairs are conducted by semi-autonomous vice-presidents, who, since they report to the president and request approval of actions considered advisable, are more directly in charge of day-to-day policy-making than the president. This would perhaps be less serious if administration by vice-presidents were confined to business policy. But often the educational policies are administered in the same fashion, and the New President, a man who has not grown up in the hard world of faculty controversy and the hopeful world of faculty planning, is shut away from the knowledge he needs in order to decide whether or not the project of his vice-president or dean is one to which he should commit his university. With the internal life of the university in the hands of administrative assistants, deans, and departmental chairmen, and the external life directed by the ultimate necessities of finance, with its dependence upon trustee, legislative, and public approval, the New President occupies the position of a mirror which merely reflects the existing realities of the university and of society.

It is often said, in justification of the new Presidential Man, that his efforts on behalf of public relations, fund-raising, business management, and efficiency are needed so that the faculty and students can gain the financial backing so essential for the improvement of the quality of education. Therefore, a businessman or administrator as such, who is not a scholar, a scientist, a humanist, or an intellectual, is better equipped for the task.

This argument contains a dangerous fallacy in its separation of financial policymaking from educational policy-making. The former has great control over the latter. The administrator of a business organization can switch from making rubber tires to making plastic cups without endangering the new business he is entering, since there are experts in plastic whom he can employ to advise him on production, and the product is standard. But in the case of education, so much depends upon the philosophy of those in control, which in turn sums up the values by which decisions are made, that the college administrator who is inexperienced in the processes and subtleties of the educational system has no clue to the kind of advice he should be seeking, and the kind of expert he should be hiring.

For ultimately, in university life, the quality of the institution depends upon the character and values of the persons who are appointed to the administration and faculty. This in turn determines the qualities of the intellectual, moral, and social environment into which the students come, and thus, with the meshing of student qualities and faculty leadership, determines primarily the values, ideals, and development of the students themselves.

THE PRESIDENT'S JOB IN MAKING APPOINTMENTS

Central in this process is the kind of leadership which the president and administrative officers can give by the appointments which they make to the university. In the long run the educational philosophy of the institution is created by these individuals no matter what views are held by the president or the dean.

The conceptual framework of any educational philosophy is empty until filled with the personal content of each teacher working with each other teacher, and each student. The work of President Lowell, President Harper, President Gilman, President Wilbur, or President Van Hise was to hold clearly in mind a set of ideals and values to be achieved, and then to bring to the university the kind of men and women who were devoted to achieving those values. In the case of the new Presidential Man, the capacity for discrimination among ideals and values is of necessity under developed through lack of severe intellectual discipline and experience of rigorous valuing, and consequently the grasp of criteria by which to choose men and women who will carry out values and ideals is bound to be weak.

Consider, for example, the problem of the administrative president in choosing his aides who will make educational policy. The lack of intimate understanding of conflicting educational philosophies, the lack of experience in determining quality of intellect, scholarship, and teaching ability, and the sheer lack of knowledge of the way in which faculty decisions and reactions to decisions come about, make it necessary for the New President to rely upon the recommendations of those whom he trusts, either inside or outside his own university. But the necessary equipment and experience to choose these initial advisers is also lacking, since it is necessary to know what kind of advice is most adequate, relevant, and helpful before making the initial decision as to whose advice must count for the most. In actual practice, this means that decisions regarding key administrative posts which the president must make in order to carry out any clear educational aim are made (1) by the weight of opinion produced by non-faculty advisers, other presidents, business acquaintances, trustees, administrators, or by the general record and reputation of the appointee; (2) by the cancelling-out of faculty and administrative opinion by one group as against another group in the forces operating within the university; or (3) by intuition, "a knowledge of men," or by a personal preference for one of the few persons in university life whom the administrator knows.

These various factors overlap, and many other factors enter into the decisions made. But the primary fact emerges that without the knowledge and experience which only a member of the community of scholars can have, the administrator is ill equipped to choose wisely among the educational policy-makers he brings to aid him. He cannot make the daring appointment, he has no instruments to detect in the untried and the unrecognized those qualities of promise which will eventually grow to greatness. The appointments will be safe, unimaginative, usually from inside the institution.

The President's Job in Policy-Making

Nor is this President equipped to choose wisely among all the ideas, projects, and suggestions made by the faculty and administrative aides around him. When added to the inevitable lack in knowledge of an educational philosophy, this means that the vitality of leadership and the sense of direction which each university needs is replaced by a kind of general momentum towards unclear goals, a momentum which is the combination of all the institutional forces at work, both inside the university and outside it in society.

This is not to say that American education is unable to advance unless all educational administrators are scholars or scientists. Education will advance one way or another. It is to say, however, that American education will not provide leadership to society if the administration is in the hands of business managers and men chosen not for their ideas and ideals in education, but for their record of competence in administration.

This lack of leadership both in the intellectual life of the university and in the clarification of issues in the society around it is particularly dangerous in our time in America. We search with difficulty for clarity of thought in public figures: The Senators, Congressmen, and political leaders are committed to party projects and opportunities. Leaders of business enterprise are largely committed to the corporate interests of a specific enterprise. The military leaders cannot be expected to reach sensitive and informed conclusions upon social issues. The institutions of organized religion are not able to produce in large measure the quality of hard-headed social criticism needed for contemporary life. By a kind of default, the editorial writers of weekly magazines, the radio commentators, the novelists and writers, Mr. Herbert Hoover, and the university presidents are those who have been thrust into the task of social comment, since, in each case, they represent institutions of recognized status, are in the role of observer rather more than of special-interest participants, and have special opportunity for making public statements on current affairs and moral values.

In this situation it is of enormous importance that the educational leadership of the country be in the hands of those whose continual concern has been to study closely the place of knowledge, scholarship, and liberal values in contemporary civilization, and whose natural sympathies and attitudes afe with the enquiring mind and the research into truth. It is an intellectual and moral stance we look for, one which is on guard against the attack by society upon the liberal values which make civilization itself worth having, and which is ready to protect society from its own vices and weaknesses. It is a stance, not only of protection, but of readiness to aid and promote ideas for the improvement of contemporary life.

These are necessities for the vitality of public statement and leadership in America, and are not to be found in the new Presidential Man, who, having absorbed the conventions and clichés of an uncriticized world, is capable only of repeating them with an air of solemnity whenever the occasion is provided. Ghost-writers, whether from the faculty or from the public relations department, are of help only in preventing the grosser errors which might betray an intellectually sterile past. On the other hand, it should not be assumed that the educational administrator is a thinker whose role it is to state educational propositions which it is then the duty of his colleagues and of society to carry out. No philosophical concept or philosophy of education ever appears in actual existence as a pure form. No matter how an educator tries, if he is innocent enough to try, he cannot build an educational institution upon preconceptions which then become exactly mirrored in reality. In the relation of ideas to life, life dominates and makes over ideas until they are different from their conceptual purity in the philosopher's mind. Only by a severe effort at isolation from life and social existence can a philosopher or administrator avoid shifting the ground and content of his knowledge to conform to the processes of life itself. He must, to some extent, blind himself to reality in order to retain conceptual purity.

In the case of colleges and universities, the students and faculty make short work of the purity or pretension of abstract educational ideas. Any idea for education, except perhaps that of a military academy, becomes so modified in practice by the character of the individuals who make up the institution that occasionally the idea becomes transformed into its opposite simply by the fact that it is given form by human beings who think, believe, and act in particular ways, and recreate all ideas as they go along. Accordingly, there are progressive schools which are actually rigid, there are traditional schools with flexible methods, there are democratic colleges full of undemocratic customs.

THE PEOPLE MAKE POLICY IN ACTION

It is, therefore, dangerous to talk too much about philosophy unless we think constantly of the people who hold philosophies and what they do with them, either in or out of school. It is also dangerous to think that any educational aim is ever realized simply by making an institution according to a philosophy, and putting young people into it. The test must always be, what are the values and attitudes of the faculty and the students, and to what extent do these values enrich the life of the individual and of the society of which he is a part?

The total aim of higher education is to induce certain attitudes and values, principal among which is the valuing of knowledge as personally significant and socially useful. Those who want to know, know. The area and content of their knowledge varies, but they know if they want to, they know the things they want to know, and, in general, they will do the things they want to do.

The task of the school or college therefore is to transform the wanting to those areas of human life connected with higher values, that is, values reached by a process of intellectual, emotional, and moral discrimination. The quality of any college, its philosophy and its practices, can be measured by whether or not the higher values are so imbedded in the day-to-day life of the community that they are absorbed unconsciously, as well as consciously, into the thinking, feeling, and acting of the individual student, and whether or not these values do in fact enrich the life of the individual and, through him, the lives of others. To meet this test is the responsibility of the faculty, in whom the ideals must be embodied if they are to be communicated at all. There are many ways of giving liberal ideals their natural setting, in which the experiences of the individual student can develop in him a love of knowledge, a desire to serve others by its use, and an understanding of the role of the liberal individual in the modern world.

The ideal is to make an institution in which every person involved shares the common aims, and each person is committed to reaching it. If the aim is to provide instruction in subjects to students at a certain price, emphasis on the part of the faculty and administration is placed upon the business arrangements of the university. The students pay for slabs of subject-matter, and take them off as quickly as they can in order to be ready for a job which pays well. The faculty dispenses the subject-matter at as high a price as the competitive bidding of the current faculty market can produce, and carries on its own research in order to become a more attractive piece of academic merchandise in the eyes of the purchasing agents or deans. The president's role is therefore to buy as much instructional talent for as little as possible, to manage the hotel and auxiliary enterprises of sport and housing, and to report to the board of trustees on the success of the venture as measured in terms of numbers of customers served, increased public recognition, and amount of money in the bank. There is no basic difference between this and any other business project in American society. A group of owners want something done and they hire people to do it. They dispense a standard product, through text-books, lectures, and the credit system.

Academic Rank By Function

To a certain extent, this kind of administrative organization is unavoidable. A large university with its complex of professional schools, vocational training, liberal arts, crowded student body, and limited faculty numbers, must make some procedural arrangements if the institution is to work at all. In the case of the liberal arts college, however, which is the intellectual and moral center of a university, or in the case of an independent institution without professional schools around it, the aim lends itself more easily to a truly democratic system of administration. The only limit upon democracy here is the extent to which a particular community can make it work successfully. The aim of such a college is to provide a free and congenial environment in which the young and their teachers can work together at the task of recreating and increasing knowledge and values. This means that each member of the community has something to contribute towards that increase, either by learning or by teaching others. There is, therefore, no administrative reason why there need be a hierarchy of faculty, administration, department chairmen, trustees, president, or students. There is only need for assignment of function so that each person involved may be able to do the most that he can for the whole community, as he proceeds with the fulfillment of his own abilities and desires.

The most recent example of a democratic institutional framework built around a common aim is that of the research units formed during the war and after for advanced research in atomic energy, physics, and allied sciences. Here the common aim is to press forward in research and discovery, and the teaching and learning are universally shared by each member of the organization at whatever stage in his own development he may have reached. Here is again the community of the learned, to whom students come to advance their own knowledge and the general knowledge of the world. Each member of the research unit is actually committed to the general aim, and it would be foolish to arrange a hierarchy of talent except in terms of the contribution and function of the individual members. Two important consequences follow immediately. It is essential to have the administration of the unit in the hands of a person who is respected in his profession by the members of the group. It is essential that policy decisions be made as a result of consultation and conference with those in the group who have relevant knowledge and insight, no matter whether the individual be a senior or a junior member of the unit in either years or academic status. A third consequence usually follows. It is essential that the research unit be of a size which lends itself to participation in policy-making, and that the total organization of research be decentralized when the laboratory situation becomes expanded.

The analogy with the college of liberal arts is close. Each person who comes to the college to teach and to learn needs to feel that he is sharing in a common aim, and that he is coming to a center of learning in which the total effort of the community is directed to making fresh discoveries. These discoveries will vary from person to person according to the amount of energy, talent, and imagination which the individual can muster. No contribution is too small, whether it consists of a small project on frogs by a student of biology or a joint study of economic trends by the social science faculty. It is the presence of this aim as a consciously held value for students and faculty which transforms an institution for dispensing subjects into a lively community of teachers and students.

THE PRESIDENT'S JOB AS EXECUTIVE

The role of the president in this institution is to give every help he can to the release of the existing and potential talents of the faculty and student body. His own satisfaction must come from the things which the students and faculty accomplish. He may also contribute what he knows and what he can do as a teacher, administrator, and student of education. When he speaks in public about education or about his college, his remarks should come as a result of close acquaintance with the ideas and beliefs of the students and faculty with whom he associates, he should go to school to his own colleagues, who, because they are teaching and because they spend more time with students and with educational ideas in practice, know more about education than he. When the president makes a statement about American education or the American student, as he can scarcely avoid doing on occasion, he should ask himself, "Which particular parts of American education are you talking about, and what does it mean as far as your college is concerned?" "Which American students do you mean, what are their names, would they agree that they think and act the way you say they do?" In this sense, the college is a continuing course of instruction for the president, as well as a laboratory for any ideas which he and his colleagues may have for the improvement of education. If he regards it in such a light, his own education is improved and he is kept closely in touch with the realities of contemporary thought.

The administration of a college by a president is a responsibility delegated to him by a governing body of trustees, regents, or directors. It is because of the similarity in structure between this situation and the usual corporation or business that often the role of the president is misconstrued in the public mind, and occasionally in the minds of trustees themselves. The final control of the college must be in the hands of one or another corporate body, since the authorities of the state who charter educational institutions must fix the responsibility. This body could best be chosen by faculty members and students themselves if the project began *de novo*. However, the control of the governing body is not that of a board of directors which has employed a manager to serve its interests. It is the control of men and women who feel that as citizens they have a responsibility to share actively in the development of higher education, and who agree to put their energies into an institution designed for that purpose. They are the guardians of the welfare of the college, the faculty, and the students, and appoint a president to give it the management which the community needs. The president is therefore responsible to his colleagues in the board of trustees and to his colleagues in the faculty for the advance of the institution by the kind of joint planning they can all do together, with the advice and help of the students. When he reports to the board, he is explaining for the benefit of the whole community the progress which they have all made together.

The actual administration of a college requires a great deal of physical and emotional energy. The luxuries of impatience, annoyance, spontaneous comment, sudden enthusiasms, hates, personal taste, discouragement, and weariness are the exclusive privilege of the faculty and students and not to be enjoyed by the president. Letters which one might write as a faculty member to a colleague become suddenly charged with hidden meanings when written on the letterhead of the president's office. Casual remarks made in the middle of a noisy dinner party abruptly become the View of the Administration. This has a chastening effect upon the administrator, and may improve him if he can live through it without becoming circumspect.

THE PRESIDENT AS CHAIRMAN OF TEACHERS

Since the aim of the college is the creation of a free community in which liberal values can be achieved in daily life, each part of the community must be self-governing and must be related to every part in the mutual government of the whole. This means that the student body must be given responsibility for governing its own affairs, not only in the trivialities of social decorum, but in the basic policies affecting life on the campus, the conduct of student discipline, the shape of the curriculum, and the direction in which the college is moving. The administrative staff and employees must also be self-governng, with representation in the policy-making of the institution, either through union delegates or through committees organized within the college system. The faculty, through its own elected committees and through its representation on the board of trustees, must be self-governing and must make faculty policy, in cooperation with the administrative officers of the college. There is no educational reason why appointments to the faculty need to be approved by a board of trustees. If the appointments continually create situations which the trustees feel are detrimental to the college, either the president can be asked to resign or those trustees who disapprove most strongly can themselves resign, since the college in that case would not be carrying out the values of the trustee in question.

The president, in this system, performs the role of chairman of a committee of the whole. He is a faculty member with additional responsibilities. In making decisions, he is not deciding for himself what is best for everyone, but he is choosing from the many alternatives which are presented to him that alternative which, in the view of his student, trustee, and faculty associates and seen in the context of his own experience, shows most promise of contributing to the total aim of the community. His power, in any radically democratic organization, depends upon the trust which his associates place in him, a trust which either develops or not on the basis of the daily decisions which he makes throughout each year. His power is greatest when he never uses it. When he presents a point of view regarding university policy, it must be one whose strength he can estimate with some accuracy as far as the support it may receive within the university itself. It must be one which he is prepared to argue on its merits, not as a presidential position from which there is no retreat. His best means of achieving the leadership his institution needs is to discover those of his colleagues who agree with the value of the specific projects which seem to him desirable, and leave it in the hands of those individuals and their associates to carry it out.

In every university there are beliefs and convictions held by the faculty about society, human nature, education and human life, and there are unstated attitudes and tendencies which have constant bearing upon daily affairs. These make up the content of the institutional life and, in many cases, do not receive formulation except in honorific terms at convocations and commencement ceremonies. The leader in education is the president or dean who can formulate these convictions and the things unsaid in a way which can give direction and clarity to the pattern of events which are presently occurring.

No idea or set of ideas belongs to the president, even though he may sometimes be the first to make suggestions. Ideas belong to those who have the responsibility for carrying them out, and those who make the commitment and spend the energy in doing so. The president may find that a great many things which seemed to be of enormous significance when written in a memorandum become much less so when placed in the middle of faculty discussion. But ultimately, the success of any program lies in whether or not there are individual human beings who believe in it and will work for it.

Strong and Weak Presidents

This is the point at which it is necessary to discuss the strong and the weak president. We have all known institutions in which the weakness, incompetence, amiability, insensitivity, or arrogance of a president has created a situation in which the faculty has begun to organize itself so strongly that the president is put in chains. This is usually desirable, although occasionally unjust and disastrous to the institution. Continuous amiability in a president and the desire to have no trouble leads to a mediocrity in the intellectual and social environment of any college. Naturally, those with strong views or interest in and talent for faculty intrigue will rise to the occasion and seize power, either directly or indirectly. It is desirable that this should happen in most cases, since only by such means will sufficient energy be mustered to divide the faculty and to take specific action in one way or another.

The first necessity for the institution and its president is thus a deep and clearly held belief in its aim. If the college is conceived as a place where new discoveries are made, new ways of thinking are tried, and new modes of education are put to the test, in short, if the college is genuinely devoted to a search for truth, then the president must be a man who, in coming to the college, is willing to devote himself to achieving that purpose. If he carries out that commitment, his faculty will forgive him many of his errors and support his general effort. He himself will be careful to bring faculty and administrative colleagues around him who conceive their role in the institution to be that of carrying out the improvement of education for the students and faculty. The criterion by which he and his faculty will judge policy decisions will then be, How will this action affect the individual student? What will be its effect on the individual faculty member? Will it further the freedom and security of the whole community? Will it increase the quality of life in the community? Will it help to establish better ways of teaching and learning?

These are questions which are seldom raised in the formation of educational policy. When raised, they will cut through the departmental, personal, and hierarchical interests of the faculty, and putting a problem out in the open where it may be seen as an aid or a hindrance to the aim of the institution will help to remove the obstacles to solution. The strength of the president is therefore directly proportional to the way in which he can hold clearly in mind the goals of the institution, the way he can ask and receive the help of his colleagues in carrying out those goals, and the chance he provides for every student, faculty member, trustee, and employee of the institution to move the institution towards its aim.

Strong and Weak College Communities

The strength of the institution itself depends solely upon the way in which each individual in this community of interested people will put his own strength at the service of the ideal. This can only happen through the experience in each of a feeling of belonging to a significant community in a larger society, and a feeling of respect for the college and for himself as a part of it. This, in turn, can only happen if there exists, in fact, a serious intellectual environment in which policy discussions concern serious educational and social issues and not inconsequential details involving departmental prerogatives and quantities of subject-matter.

The making of ends and means must be a continual process with which the faculty as a whole and its separate committees are concerned from month to month and year to year. Curriculum planning, for example, must not be a matter of adding and subtracting subjects, but a matter of raising questions as to whether or not certain means and ends in the work of teachers with students are those which, upon close examination, show promise of educational advance.

The curriculum committee itself should not be an isolated group of talking planners, but should be a research group which consults students and teachers everywhere throughout the college in order to discover exactly how the means and ends are conceived in the actual process of education. Similarly the faculty admissions committee should be a research body which constantly evaluates its criteria and the results of those criteria in selecting students and educating them. It too should be closely in touch with teachers throughout the college in order to discover the evaluations which teachers make of the work of those students admitted. Through the whole college there must be constant reference to the views of students and the educational results which in their opinion are being achieved by the program. Not only must there be an opportunity for consultation with students upon all important issues, but there must be policy-making committees among them with power to recommend and act, and responsibility for reporting back to the student body and faculty.

To this end, a radically democratic community, which is perhaps only possible in the world of learning, is an instrument of morale and efficiency as much as a moral ideal. There will be no shared democratic experience until faculty and students are given the freedom and power and responsibility for making policies with the aid of the president, dean, and administrative officers. The usual chart of organization has to be redrawn and has to replace the chain-of-command concept with the president at the top center and linked to the lesser mortals contained in squares marked Students, Faculty, Employees, and so on, with a movable set of representatives who are sometimes at the top, sometimes at the bottom, side, or middle of the framework. The process is organic, and not linear.

In this system the governing body of trustees, regents, or directors, by a grant of powers, confers upon the college community the right of self-government and reserves to itself the final responsibility for the welfare and stability of the institution. The board contains a diversity of public representation from social, educational, and economic groups, with specific representation from faculty and alumnae and access to student opinion. Most of the working committees of the board should be joint faculty-trustee committees.

Within the college community, elected committees should conduct the basic administration with an executive officer in charge of the office work. Appointments, dismissals, salary increases, and other matters should be the final responsibility of the president, who will work with the dean and a small committee elected by the faculty to advise him on particular cases. All information which is available to the president should be made available to the committee. The majority approval of individual appointments by the entire faculty is neither a desirable nor a necessary democratic procedure. The fact that all opinions of all faculty members must be reconciled in the light of information which will inevitably be inadequate makes it unlikely that this procedure can work best for the total interest of the college. The faculty will make general policy upon which individual cases may be decided, but the actual decisions in this field must be made by a few carefully elected representatives who respect the integrity of the committee's function and who are responsible to their colleages for the individual welfare of each.

The question of status of faculty members will thus be decided not in terms of their position in a hierarchy of professors, associates, assistants, and instructors—there will be no formal rank—but in terms of the functions in the community. This function will be a decision reached partly by faculty election of committee members and partly by the views of the administration as to which individuals can be most helpful either formally as college officials or informally as advisers.

Since the aim of the college is to approach new discovery from many points of view, the departmental system, by which knowledge is institutionally manufactured in segments, must be radically modified. The departmental chairman, who is conventionally conceived as the third unit in a chain of command linked to the president and dean, must now be placed in a situation analogous to the chairman of a committee of equals who are all devoted to a common end, the advancement of learning in the students and the methods and content of their education. The newest arrival to the department could thus be chairman if his talent for that administrative work were clear. The chairman is responsible for his group as a community in the same way as the president is responsible for the morale and advancement of the whole institution.

Emphasis must be placed, in departmental planning, upon the needs and abilities of the individual student, and the subject-matter fields must be divided and administered in terms of the kind of knowledge which seems most likely to achieve the greatest development of each student.

This will eventually mean the disappearance of departments as such, since it entails an emphasis upon the continuous study of the progress of students in achieving the ideals of the educational program, and an emphasis upon the diversity of ways in which each member of the faculty can work out his own mode of teaching his own courses. The departmental courses which present the faculty member with a syllabus will be discarded and will be replaced by a system in which the individual teacher is free to deal with his students in terms of his own knowledge and the aim of the college program. Conferences will be held among teachers who are dealing with similar groups of students to pool ideas, suggestions, and insights, all of which may be helpful to the improvement of the separate courses. Out of this will emerge a general pattern of courses, but the pattern will be one created by the empirical method, and will be one which changes and reforms in the light of new experience from every quarter. In other words, the organization of knowledge into a vital curriculum adapted to the needs and abilities of the students and the capacities of the faculty is the construction of an intellectual democracy. The educational planning within each unit of the university structure will exhibit the characteristics of the research unit or group of inquiring scholars, who, in looking to each other for help in making progress and in working out particular ways of teaching and learning which may serve as examples, are fulfilling both an intellectual and a moral function at the same time. In this way the vitality of teaching and learning is in part assured, since the teacher will be responsible, not to a departmental chairman or a dean, but to the aim of improving the educational system. There is no other way to stimulate a continuing interest in the college policies and in teaching processes than by giving to each teacher the freedom to experiment and the responsibility for improving the institution. The work of each teacher will then be enriched by the work of every other.

Some Conditions of Democratic Administration

There are colleges fortunate in the free and flexible situation in which teachers can work, colleges which are radically democratic in theory and constitution, and interesting and productive in practice. I am pleased to say that the institution I represent is one of these. Its system contains the elements listed above, and a number of others which it is not the concern of this chapter to discuss. Some of the informality and ease of communication of our life in the college is possible because we are a small and closely knit community. Some of the experiments in democracy which we are able to make are due to the fact that the Constitution set down by the founders was expressly designed to foster a democratic community of students and teachers. But most of the practices which are in effect at the college are not those assured by the Constitution, but those preferred by individuals and founded upon precedent.

As institutions grow in size, and as the operational details of the organization grow in number, the distance between the administration on the one hand and the faculty and students on the other is likely to assume the proportions of a gulf. The president becomes more and more isolated from his students and his faculty the larger his university becomes. The deans, administrative officers, and departmental chairmen actually stand between him and his proper business of conducting education. This situation can only be remedied by the initiative of the president. He must retain close connection with the students and the faculty by whatever means can be devised. In the case of President Conant, this has taken the form of teaching classes in science; in the case of President Stoddard, conferences with faculty and students upon university policy. The appointment of new members of departments, divisions, or administrative units must always be a matter for close scrutiny by the president. He should know from first-hand experience the kind of person who is being appointed by those to whom he has delegated authority. He should foster the notion in the minds of each faculty member that, as far as the students are concerned, each professor is his own college president, with authority to conduct their education in a way mutually congenial to the teacher and the student.

The size of the institution in this regard is not an ultimately controlling factor. The system of democratic custom can be built by a president who provides the symbol for that system by the way in which he shares in the life of the institution. He cannot do this single-handed, nor as a crusader for his own doctrinal democracy. He can do it by example, by appointment, by indirection, by a series of decisions which loosen up the rigidities of the usual institutional patterns. He will find support for such reform in any institution, if for no other reason than the law of averages. The degree of his success will depend upon the qualities of the colleagues with whom he works, the sincerity of his own democratic purposes, and the skill he can develop in the daily administration of the institution. His chances of success are greatest when he conceives of himself as the executive officer of a community of scholars, and as one determining factor in the organic process of change which occurs in social institutions.

CHAPTER IV

THE NATURE AND FUNCTION
OF DEMOCRATIC ADMINISTRATION

H. GORDON HULLFISH

Ohio State University

Scope of the Problem

THE task of keeping the American college or university on a high level of administrative effectiveness is not easily performed. In some of its parts the task appears as little more than a business operation. The need for making buildings, books, research materials, office services, and the like available in ways that use financial resources without waste is an instance of business management. Other parts of the task, however, are largely political. Financial support is not merely given; it has to be gained. The merit of the administrator's case, which seems to be the reasonable base on which to request financial support, may turn out to have no essential bearing on the extent of support achieved. The selfishness or stupidity of a single legislator or donor, or the desire on the part of either to play God, can jeopardize the most carefully prepared case. The administrator has to be sufficiently the politician to deal successfully with the political forces related to the maintenance of institutional health and yet retain his integrity both as a representative of the educational profession and as a person.

Always, of course, the administrative task in its totality is moral. The relationships of human beings are affected by all administrative decisions. This fact should never be forgotten. Callousness here can make a shambles of the intellectual enterprise, removing the possibility that those who should be above arbitrary restriction will ever feel free to play out the last thread of an idea to see what next steps intelligence suggests in the scholarly enterprises for which they are responsible. Professors are affected no less than others who engage in the human enterprise by the conditions of the field within which they grow and wherein they perform their services. This is a lesson that mankind has surely, if slowly, learned. The valuing men do is conditioned by the quality of the human associations within which the valuing is done. All adminustrative problems arise in relationship to it and return to it as solutions are finally tested against the nature of the human consequences to which they lead.

The conclusion has slowly emerged on campus after campus that higher education in a democracy is morally obligated to gain its character through its exemplification of the spirit of the democratic aspiration. This does not represent the emergence of simple sentimentality. What is involved is the recognition that the language of democracy is as empty as is the language of any other way of life when it has no meaningful rooting in the relationships of men who use it. The administration of our colleges and universities is not in the hands of those who possess "a completed democracy" which it is theirs to give or withhold as they wish. All who are *within* an institution are at this point *of* it. The creation of democratic relationships is a conjoint task but, and this is hard to overemphasize, the administration is in a strategic position. Whatever may be its wish, it does exercise leadership by the simple fact of designation. It may wield power, as power, and thus fail, even though judged to be efficient by what is recorded on the budget sheets; or it may build power, the power of understanding, as it helps men find their responsible place in shared effort.

It would be folly to suggest that this statement of the problem forces to the fore a single, or simple, solution. The situation is quite otherwise. It is true that certain practices may at once be seen to be preferable to others, yet we immediately realize that practice in itself may remain unenlightened routine. Moreover, implicit in our problem is the larger problem of the meaning of the democratic aspiration itself.

An administration that accepts its responsibility as an instrument of the democratic aspiration may discover, as it acts with full integrity, that faculty members or students view democracy in differing terms. This may be a cause for disappointment; it is not, however, an occasion for despair. Nowhere more than in colleges and universities should we look forward to advance than when ideas are in conflict. The essence of higher education and, indeed, of democracy, is found in the pooling of differing ideas for the purpose of seeking better ones. If, then, we start where we are, and not as if the sudden insight of a leader would settle the matter, we shall build from the considerable experience we have already had.

Our institutions of higher learning have their being within a democratic culture and, though they may not have worked out all the implications of this fact, they are not unaffected by it. We have at least a vague sense that democracy should be reflected in the administrative pattern. It is for this reason that some of us reach for complete freedom for ourselves. Other citizens do this, too. It is for this reason that others of us insist upon having a voice in all decisions, perhaps even in taking a vote to bring the decisions into being. These, too, have their counterparts in the citizenry at large. Finally, it is for this reason that most of us move uncertainly over a middle ground, not quite clear what it is that democracy does mean in institutional arrangements. We share the confusion of citizens generally.

Our institutions of higher learning are not, of course, unique in their inability to organize themselves in democratic terms. Educational institutions generally fall short on this score, as do other institutions. We have felt that in the doing of our jobs—organizing labor and improving the conditions of work, advancing the industrial process and keeping the profit margins safe, extending educational services and admitting increasing numbers of students—we were serving democracy well. And so, in general, we were. We made our life a vigorous life, in which more and more people had an opportunity to share. It is this fact which lies behind our present desire to have our institutions serve democracy further. We are striving now to carry forward *at the conscious level* what we have heretofore achieved, somewhat unreflectively, within the momentum of our growth. We cannot leave our further gains to chance.[1]

The present need of our institutions of higher learning is to illustrate the personal and social differences which result when human effort is illuminated by democratic insights. Those who administer these institutions have, then, a two fold task. They must, first, understand what values are critical values within the democratic aspiration; they must, second, experiment in the daily administrative acts in which they engage to discover appropriate ways of giving these values positive work to do in the transformation of institutional operations.[2] This may seem to be a large order. It is, and for a specific reason. The habits and attitudes of individual administrators are involved. This carries us to the moral level, to the choice among consequences of routine and deliberate acts as these have meaning for human devel-

[1] "The Functions of the Faculty in the Administrative Process," by H. Gordon Hullfish, in Chap. VIII, *The Administration of Higher Institutions Under Changing Conditions*, p. 74, Norman Burns, editor (Proceedings of the Institute for Administrative Officers of Higher Institutions, 1947).

[2] Chapter III has shown, for instance, the way in which group activities may be directed so that a high degree of democratic valuing will be a consequence of the shared effort to solve common problems.

opment. "We have," as John Dewey has pointed out,[3] "advanced far enough to say that democracy is a way of life. We have yet to realize that it is a way of personal life and one which provides a moral standard for personal conduct." Basically, then, the administrative task is one of creating on each campus those human relationships which have the central and unifying purpose of freeing the human personality. The free man is, in truth, the authentic symbol of the democratic aspiration. Since man, however, becomes free through interaction with his fellows, not in isolation from them, there are characteristics of the human relationship which are equally the authentic representation of this aspiration. It is these characteristics to which an administration may turn as it seeks essential direction for the reconstruction of its practices.

To begin with, more is at issue than the mere fact of association of men to men. We cannot escape association with others, even in the best planned ivory tower; but association, as such, tells us little at this point. Ours is not a quest for that which is but for that which lies yet ahead. Our experience, to be sure, provides us with our hunches. Not all association is, from the point of view of the free man, good. Some men are crushed in association; others are released. We know that what happens to men in association can be planned by other men; hence, we know further that we are confronted now by the social need to learn to plan in the interest of all men. The democratic aspiration has arisen within the facts of experience; it represents, however, an ideal transformation of that experience.

That there are many ways in which to characterize the transformation to which the democratic aspiration points is all too obvious. This fact can be disturbing under certain

[3] *Freedom and Culture,* by John Dewey, p. 130 (New York: G. P. Putnam's Sons, 1939).

circumstances, yet it is suggestive. The concept is little more than a charge to men to fill in its meaning. It provides an occasion for finding out what it is that is needed in a given situation to make freedom available there. It is, as an abstraction, a growing edge in the field of human relationships. It suggests, it does not dictate. It calls upon intelligence, not upon rules. It suggests principles of interaction, not formal patterns of association. It frees those, in short, who seek freedom.

PRINCIPLES OF DEMOCRATIC ADMINISTRATION

The essential principles that flow from the acceptance of the democratic aspiration, so far as gaining insight into the nature and function of democratic administration is concerned, are few in number. They are, however, critical; critical, in the sense that to neglect them is to neglect an opportunity to foster the democratic aspiration itself. These principles are:

the principle of free intelligence
The life of a group is enriched in exact relationship to the secure knowledge on the part of each individual that the intelligence counts and will be respected, and to the degree that each individual becomes disciplined in bringing his intelligence to bear significantly upon the group enterprise.

the principle of participation
No individual is free who is cut off from his group. This is true in the world at large; it is true on the campus. It is as true of a president or dean who builds his world behind an administrative door as it is of a young instructor who, by precedent, is never consulted in matters of institutional policy.

the principle of individuality
Each individual is uniquely an individual. His interests are particular interests, and his abilities are special abilities. These differences are, in associated life, sources of potential strength, The life of the group will suffer where they are permitted to degenerate into divisive idiosyncrasies; and, too, so will the lives of individuals.

The principles of cooperation

In the final analysis individual men become free as they achieve ways of sharing in the task of creating the social conditions within which the free working of intelligence on the part of individuals who take part in conjoint activities without being coerced to do so is prized. Such men learn, too, to value the particular strength of each individual man.

There is, of course, an interrelatedness among these principles. Each represents a specific way within a total field of interaction of advancing a common aspiration. Moreover, one does not stand above another in hierarchical manner. Each asks for consideration in each situation where a decision is reached as to how the human enterprise is to go forward. Each offers itself as a tool that will help free men be wise in decision. Each, to state the matter somewhat differently, represents an aspect of a directing human purpose. Each, finally, may be set down by the administrator as *a direction flag* within the total of his operations.

Free Intelligence. Specifically, where *the principle of free intelligence* is denied, there can be no college or university worthy of the name. One might say, without fear of serious challenge, that the essence of the administrative function is to make it possible for a free intelligence to do its maximum work. We have seen institutions in this country fall short of greatness because a weak, or at the very best, an ignorant, administration has failed to honor this principle. We have observed administrators as they have, in moments of local, regional, or national hysteria, rationalized their failures to let the public understand the implications of the social function of higher education in a democracy and why it is that selfish interests, individual or institutional in character, must not be allowed to wall off the intellectual life. More seriously, we have observed administrators who have so far fallen from grace as to become participants in ill-advised and unwarranted witch hunts. Of these nothing more need be said.

Fortunately, there have been courageous administrators in higher education. There are institutions, therefore, both private and public, that have stood fast as aggressive guardians of the right to deal with ideas freely.

There are specific ways in which the principle of free intelligence can be worked into institutional life. On every administrative level, from the office of the president to the desks of departmental chairmen, there is occasion in daily word and deed to honor the principle. It will bear upon such matters as the selection and use of books, the selection of new staff members, the policies used in giving advances in rank and salary, the practices followed when faculty members accept their responsibilities as citizens and engage in the social actions appropriate to the fulfillment of these responsibilities, and the attitudes expressed toward the publication of research studies that show to be false specific claims made by individuals or groups that stand to profit by holding their claims above scrutiny.

Each of these matters may arise at a given time in a special form. When this is so, the function of intelligence is to discover what is then appropriate to do, what the specific nature of the situation is. But this gives no warrant to an administration to live from situation to situation without guiding principle. A firm statement of policy is a first institutional need. A wise president will seek faculty aid in the formulation of this policy. A strong president will then stand on it, protecting it against sabotage either from within or from without the institution. He will urge it upon his board of control for adoption as official policy; and he may well doubt the advisability of remaining in office should this request be refused in a manner that places in jeopardy the free working of intelligence on his campus.

The importance of these considerations is not that faculty members are special creatures who need to be pampered.

As a matter of fact, the socially responsible faculty member does not seek academic freedom for himself. He seeks it because he knows that the future citizen on campus can be properly educated, and the present citizen off campus can be adequately served, only by institutions of higher education within which the principle of free intelligence is a normal expectation. Moreover, he seeks it the more earnestly today because the future of free men depends upon its cultivation, institution by institution.

The problems men now confront, the problems to which our best and most devoted intelligence must now be turned, arise from tensions and uncertainties in the field of human relationships. These problems can be solved only as fact is substituted for prejudice, as truth replaces dogma. Our present responsibility is clear. We are called upon to seek knowledge and understanding in the field of human relations with the same vigor that has been characteristic of our search in the technical fields.

The challenge before us arises from the distinctive need of our people, the need to understand the social consequences of knowledge as this is gained. It will not be easy to meet this challenge. Some will say we should not try. We reject this as unworthy of a great university. Knowledge comes to full fruition as it illuminates the lives of men. A university comes into its rightful heritage as it helps men live examined lives.

There are, then, certain quite specific tasks before us today. We shall need to stand firm administratively to our historical commitment, that the life of a university is uniquely a life in which the free interplay of idea upon idea is highly prized. *This is the distinctive democratic commitment.* No fascist or communist state dare make it.[4]

The real test of the commitment of an administration to the principle of free intelligence occurs, of course, when the going gets rough. When angry voices are raised in the land, when social organizations or institutions set out to strangle

[4] *The Responsibilities of a University*, a communication to Howard L. Bevis, President, The Ohio State University, from the Conference Committee of the Teaching Staff on the occasion of the 75th anniversary of The Ohio State University, Columbus, Ohio, October 14 and 15, 1948.

the intellectual life of others, when special interests—openly or insidiously—try to capture institutions of higher education in order to give priority to their own narrow purposes, when politicians insist upon being merely politicians—these are occasions for an administration to show its mettle. It can do nothing less in such situations than fight the good fight. And, if we may so phrase it, win, lose, or draw, the gain will be significant. A breath of fresh air will stir within academic life in general, and in a given institution specifically. Further, the citizens of a free world will understand their own aspirations better when they observe the fearless presentation of a reasoned case for higher education. Each instance of attack, in short, is an occasion for the reaffirmation of the hopes of free men and an opportunity to help these men become ever more articulate about the manner of life they seek to achieve.

Participation. At this point we may observe the essential meaning of *the principle of participation.* Each individual on campus gains his chance to achieve freedom in his own life as he finds appropriate ways in which to express his interests and capacities in relation to the total enterprise. He is thwarted and frustrated where he is unable to do so with any sense of security, when he feels always that what he does may not have the approval of those who approve the budget. It is of basic importance, therefore, in the administration of higher education, and in relation to the mental health of teachers and students, that opportunities be provided for all to be responsible participants in bringing a community life into being. A geographic location and a collection of buildings do not add up to a community. A community is an achievement, an achievement on the part of individuals who confront common problems and purposes and who pool their special talents to build on, and to build out from, the interest they share.

At the very least, therefore, sensitivity to the principle of participation on the part of an administration will lead to experimentation in administrative practice in order that ways may be found to use the varied abilities represented in any faculty and student body in the creation of a common life. Each institution has its own unique characteristics and no single pattern of practice will do for all. Indeed, the principle of participation is significant as a direction flag in the field of human relationships for the very reason that it leads away from the mechanization of relationships. The point of participation is to gain the advantage of pooled intelligence; and, in this effort, participation occurs only as individuals share responsibility when decisions are reached. It does not occur, as so many wrongly think, when committees or groups are called together for the sole purpose of approving the decisions of administrative officers. Men do not build a loyalty to an institution when their intelligence is never given an opportunity to shape decisions which have important consequences for their personal and professional lives.

It is within the concept of loyalty that we discover the final fruit of following the principle of participation in administrative practice. Men prize that which they create. When they share in a creative process, they prize together that which is representative of their common values. This does not mean that men have never prized without understanding, nor does it mean that some men have never been led to prize that which their leaders prize. These are variations on loyalty, however. They have no meaning for democratic life. Moreover, they place those who lead in a precarious position. At the first moment of distrust of the leader the center of loyalty is itself questioned. Under such circumstances there is no possibility, as there is in a democracy, of developing a loyalty to a process which invites the individual to participate in the achievement of a common life.

Thus, while it is morally right that an administration follow the principle of participation in order to insure the effective growth of each individual within the campus community, it is administratively sound, speaking now in the simple term of protective effort, to build policy and practice on the widest possible base of discussion and conference. It will then follow that faculty and students will stand loyally at the side of an administration when its acts are questioned, when the attempt is made to keep higher education from bringing intelligence to bear fully upon the problems facing our world.

Individuality and Cooperation. The principle of individuality and the principle of cooperation, no less than the others, should be held at the level of awareness as administrative action is planned and as it occurs. To begin with, staff members are selected because of the special intellectual contribution they have to make to students and to a field of knowledge. They should be given the chance to make this contribution with a minimum of difficulty. They are also selected because of their promise of effective membership in the campus community. They should be helped to realize this promise. The problem here, like all problems in the human field, is a complex one. Those who teach need time to keep abreast of the advance of knowledge in their fields and to make their own contributions to this advance. They entered teaching in the first instance because of an interest in controlling, extending, and communicating ideas. It is natural that they should spend long hours in laboratories, in libraries, in their studies. These hours are an essential part of their being. There are almost never enough of them. It is not surprising, therefore, that staff members frequently resent what appear to be administrative intrusions upon quite precious time. They are sure they are doing the work for which they are responsible; they are likely to feel that all would be well were the administration to do its work with equal faithfulness.

This feeling is warranted to a degree. The conclusion to which it points is not. The faculty and the administration in a college or university are not opposing forces. They have a common task and, while each has specific assignments appropriate to a given role, this task can be approached effectively only at the sensitive level of cooperative effort. The alternative is a competition of interests which neither can win, though each may organize and marshal sufficient pressure to stand the other off in a friendly, if uncertain, truce. We have achieved varying stages of truce in differing institutions by pursuing this alternative. It is a procedure that may properly be called *pressured cooperation*. Whatever gains result from it are temporary, subject always to the next shift in pressure. Yet it is deceptive. The gains seem otherwise. Where they are, and all things are possible in human relationships, this is because respect for the other fellow has come about in the effort to jockey for position.

Respect for the other fellow, of course, is a calculated gain on the part of those who take seriously the principle of individuality and the principle of cooperation. They do not rest their hopes on chance. In colleges and universities where there is an awareness of the part these institutions may play in the growth and development of democracy the administration, therefore, will take leadership in attempting to realize this gain fully. It will realize that faculty members do need uninterrupted stretches of time to be truly professional people. It will take this fact into account in scheduling classes, in calling staff meetings, in the demands it makes of an extracurricular nature, and the like. Above all, it will not so routinize its own practices as to reduce faculty members for portions of their day to the status of high-grade clerks.

Nor will it act arbitrarily on any score in relation to any staff member, of whatever rank.

All of this is but to say that the administration will so try to act that respect for individuality will be a quality of the experience of all in relation to it. But this is only the first step in administrative leadership regarding these principles. If no futher step is taken, the whole matter may degenerate to the level of a degrading benevolence. The next step is to foster activities, such as the formulation of the rules and regulations of the institution or the consideration of curriculum revisions, within which the honest effort is made to share wide differences of view as these exist and to achieve a common ground of advance. No institution can afford to use less than the total of the intelligence its personnel possesses; hence, no administrator is on sound ground educationally who callously turns his back upon the principle of cooperation. Moreover, no administrator has sized up the human situation properly who fails to recognize that men rise to their highest sense of individuality as they are honored in the cooperative process for the distinctive contribution they are able to make to it.

The Task Ahead

It is of course true, as the authors of this book would be the first to admit, that democracy is to be found in the administration of higher education in America. It is good that this is so. We have habits which may be used in the reconstruction of those aspects of our experience where the democratic aspiration has not thus far rooted. The basic problem to recognize, then, is that institutions of higher education are involved in the exact manner of learning process that it is their function to create for the students. Our values as they are reflected in formal statement, or as they are revealed in uncriticized practice, are now up for review. This is the essence of the educative process and all of us—administrators, teachers, and students—are impelled to engage in it wholeheartedly today. We need to know how far we can bank on the heritage of free men to carry us forward in the new world which the intelligence we would further release has already created.

Administrative leadership in higher education today confronts a critical task. It does so in relation to the rich background of experience of a people whose aspiration it has been to build a world in which the conditions of life would lead all men to prize freedom for every man. It is just such a world that administrative leadership is now called upon to create on each campus. There is intelligence available; there are devoted people. Whatever of fear there may be could be dissipated quickly by the conscientious use of the essential principles of democratic association. It is time that our colleges and universities became beacon lights along the hard trail of democratic achievement. If they fail, the glorious promise of freedom may be lost to the human scene. If they win, freedom will take its rightful starring role in the drama of a new and truly humane civilization.

CHAPTER V

SOME PRINCIPLES
OF DEMOCRATIC ASSOCIATION

HAROLD B. ALBERTY
Ohio State University

THIS chapter presents as working hypotheses some of the basic principles which characterize democratic group living, and which would have a bearing on any situation in which people live and work together. Basically, these principles are derived from an attempt to interpret the deeper meaning of the democratic way of life as it applies to group association.

The Ideals of Democratic Association

While there are many different interpretations of the ideals of democracy, perhaps most people would accept the following:

1. Democracy is a form of social organization which holds that the optimal development of the individual, of *all* individuals, represents the highest good.
2. Man achieves optimal development only through acting in concert with his fellows; each individual sensitive to the effects of his acts upon others.
3. The optimal development of all can be realized only to the extent that men have faith in intelligence as a method of solving individual and group problems.

4. The ideal of optimal development requires that all individuals who have a stake in a given enterprise share in planning and in carrying it into effect.

Upon the interpretation and application of these principles or ideals, free men are bound to disagree. Implicit in the statement is the fact of change, of continuously seeking higher levels of agreement through democratic association. The starting point, however, is the belief that human personality has dignity and worth and that the test of any proposed action ought to be: "Does it foster the richest possible living for all who will be affected by it?" As the writer has said in another connection:

This concept must not be interpreted as rugged individualism, or as *laissez faire*, for individuals in a complex technological, and there interdependent society, cannot develop through the violation or ruthless destruction of the personalities of others. The test [of democratic action] therefore is in reality a social one in the sense that human action must ultimately find its justification in the extent to which such action enhances the living of all who are touched by it. This introduces the concept of intelligence which is part and parcel of the way of life which we call democratic. We have faith in the intelligence of the common man, faith that he has the potentialities which when developed make it possible for him to solve his problems by setting up hypotheses, marshaling data, and drawing conclusions that are at least relatively free from caprice or whim. In other words, we have faith that once the ideal of enhancement of human personality is accepted, it becomes the criterion by means of which the individual tests his conclusions and arrives at plans of action. Once we deny that human beings can so act, democracy will languish and die and in its place will be substituted a form of organization in which those who have power may dictate, for better or worse, the actions of their fellowmen.[1]

[1] Quoted from *Reorganizing the High School Curriculum*, p. 35 (New York: The Macmillan Company, 1947). For two recent similar interpretations see Florence D. Cleary *et al.*, *Understanding Democracy;* and Grace Weston, *et al.*, *Democratic Citizenship and Development of Children* (Both issued by the Citizenship Education Study, Detroit Public Schools and Wayne Universitly 1949).

Upon this conception of the nature of democracy it is possible to build the principles of democratic association which should find application wherever people are associated in carrying out common purposes. Thus the principles should be applicable to the different facets of the life of a college or university—to its over-all planning and policy-making, to its classroom instruction, and to its various relationships both within and without the institution.

For purposes of this discussion, democratic association is referred to as the group process, a term which is becoming generally accepted by workers in the field of group dynamics. The meaning of the term is made clear in a recent publication:[2]

Group process . . . refers to the ends-means procedures utilized by a group of individuals thinking, discussing, planning, deciding, acting, and evaluating together for the purpose of attacking and solving a common problem. It implies the meeting and interacting of minds in face-to-face relationships in which cooperative and creative thinking takes place and action and growth ensue. *The goal of group processes is group productivity, that is, getting something done which could not be done by a single individual.*

The real focus of group processes in education is relations with or between people . . . The process creates and recreates designs which make the most of the collective judgments of the group members. The continuous mobilization of the positive elements which come out of the interaction of group members gives the group process its dynamic force and power. Its material are the ideas, feelings, and experiences of people because the group *is* people. Group processes are simply the ends-means procedures developed by a group unified by inter-dependency of behavior and by the identification of the members of the group in attacking a common problem.[2]

PRINCIPLES OF THE DEMOCRATIC GROUP PROCESS

The following principles, which grow out of the nature and interpretation of democracy, are proposed as one basis for

[2] *Group Processes in Supervision*, by Lavonne A. Hanna, Chairman, pp. 27–28 (Washington: Association for Supervision and Curriculum Development, N. E. A., 1948). (Italics in original.)

judging the extent to which an institution is practicing democracy in its various group activities.

1. *The group process is effective to the extent that concerns are shared by members of the group.*

This is another way of stating that the group process is effective only when it is utilized to solve a problem which is accepted *as a problem* by the group. If there is a job to be done which needs the cooperative thinking and planning of a group, then the process is applicable. In many instances the problem is only a problem to the status leader.[3] A good illustration of this situation is a college class in which the teacher states what to him is a problem: "What were the causes of the French Revolution?" The students merely recognize the need for satisfying the teacher by relating the facts which they may glean from the textbook. There really is nothing to discuss, no reason for an interplay of ideas. The members of the group have nothing particular at stake except the need to satisfy the requirements of the program. The situation changes completely if the group undertakes to do a radio presentation of some episode of the French Revolution, for this involves the sharing of responsibility. The writing of the script needs to be planned; the mechanical details have to be worked out; appropriate research has to be carried on, and parts have to be assigned. Of course, the status leader (teacher) may decide to do all of the planning himself and then call on the group to "cooperate," in which case there is no occasion to employ the group process at all. But if the problem is actually common to the group, and an atmosphere of permissiveness prevails, each member of the group will feel a responsibility to participate, for each has a stake in the outcome.

[3] The term *status leader* refers to the person who is charged with the official responsibility for directing the activity of a group. It might be a college president, a dean, department head, a teacher appointed to direct a certain study, or a teacher in the classroom.

2. *The group process is most effective in situations in which the leadership is shared by various members of the group.*

Each person in the group contributes to the recognized problem in terms of his special interests and competencies. In this sense the leadership passes from one member of the group to another. Kilpatrick illustrates this principle in the following quotation:[4]

. . . Many seem to think of leadership as if it were only or primarily fixed in advance, either by appointment or election or by special ability and preparation. On this basis, those proceed to divide people into two fixed groups, leaders and followers. Such a view seems inadequate, quite denied by observable facts. Actual leadership as we see it comes mostly by emergence out of a social situation. A number of people talk freely about a matter of common concern. *A* proposes a plan of action. *B* successfully voices objection and criticism. *C* then proposes a modified plan. *D*, *E*, and *F* criticize certain features of the plan. The group at this point divides, seemingly unable to agree. *G* then comes forward with a new plan that combines the desired features and avoids the evils feared. The group agrees. Here *A*, *B*, *C*, *D*, *E*, *F*, and *G* were successively leaders of the group, and each such act of leadership emerged out of the situation as it then appeared. This is democratic leadership and its success depends on—nay exactly is—an on-going process of education inherent in the situation.

If *A* had been the status leader, with the power to impose his will upon the group, he might merely have proposed his plan and had the group "discuss" it. The group might have accepted it upon the basis that the leader wanted it and had the authority to have the program carried out. Needless to say many administrators operate in this manner, sometimes in the name of democracy! This point will be discussed later.

3. *The solution of a problem arrived at through the group process is to be accepted as the "best" solution, even though*

[4] *The Community School*, Samuel Everett, editor, p. 20 (New York: D. Appleton-Century Company, 1938).

the judgment of the group is not shared by the status leader.

The files of administrators are bulging with reports of faculty groups on almost every conceivable problem. These reports have taken many hours of faculty time. They have never been acted upon, perhaps because they have not met with the approval of an administrative officer or because of the multitude of details which engulf him. This often accounts for the skepticism of faculty members when a new committee is proposed. Continuous failure to execute decisions made by faculty groups leads to eventual frustration. It is not unusual to hear teachers say: "What is the use of working on this committee? Nothing will ever come of it anyway." The democratic group process has within itself the dynamics to correct its own mistakes. In other words, decisions and plans of action are experimental or hypothetical—to be evaluated continuously and changed as new data are discovered. A curriculum developed through the democratic process, even though it may be inferior on paper to the ideal held by the leader, is a living thing worthy of respect. To fail to accept it as the "best answer" *as of that particular date* is a violation of the process by which it was created. This does not mean, of course, that the leader may not continue with the group in examining new data, and in studying the success of the venture.

4. *The group process requires that there be mutual respect for members of the group and that differences among individuals or minorities be utilized as a means of developing richer and deeper insights which will enhance the quality of the solution of the problem.*

Democracy cherishes differences among men. Rather than ruthlessly crushing out these differences, it utilizes them as data to be weighed in reaching a decision. Frequently differences are regarded as obstructions to action and those who hold them are subjected to ridicule or discipline. There is, of course, a reciprocal responsibility on the part of individuals or minorities to express their differences for the purpose of improving the quality of the contemplated decision rather than to obstruct or defeat any action whatever. Congressional filibusters are frequently illustrations of actions by minority groups which have as their direct purpose the prevention of democratic action. It would not be difficult to find similar illustrations in the activities of faculty members. As Alice Miel points out: [5]

> . . . It is well to recognize that there are differences that cannot be tolerated. Antisocial behavior on the part of some individuals makes it impossible for other individuals to play their roles creatively. The organization must protect the group from non-contributive and destructive individuals, while these persons are being helped to find a more productive role.

Obviously it would be best from the standpoint of human relations for the group to discipline its own members when differences become obstructions to progress. Perhaps, however, the status leader may have a special responsibility at this point, for he is obligated to use his leadership to protect the process. The ideal, of course, is that differences or conflicts within the group be used, as Kilpatrick points out in a quotation used earlier, to bring about a refinement or a desirable modification of the contemplated action.

5. *The effective use of the group process is one means of releasing the creative potentialities of the members of an organization.*

The purpose of the group process is, of course, the solving of a common problem. Its use must be defended on the ground that it is the only truly effective means of solving such

[5] *Changing the Curriculum,* by Alice Miel, p. 91 (New York: D. Appleton-Century Company, 1946).

problems. This fact is sometimes forgotten in discussions of "in-service" education of teachers. The inference which is easily drawn from some of these discussions is that administrators "turn over" problems to the teaching staff for the purpose of reeducating them. The assumption is that the administrator could easily solve the problem single-handed, but that "it is a good thing for the staff to struggle with it." Such an attitude is a violation of the whole theory of the process. It is nevertheless true that individual growth does take place in the process of living and working together. This concept is deeply embedded in our democratic ideals. Significant personalities cannot be developed in isolation. Rather they grow as individuals work together in terms of common concerns and interests. When a real problem is to be solved that requires the varied talents of the members of the group, growth almost inevitably takes place.

Conversely the reason why so many college faculties are "dead," is because the members have no real problems to solve that require the free interplay of ideas.[6] Each professor withdraws to his cubicle and works alone. Occasionally he "serves" on a committee at the request of some "superior" officer, bemoaning the fact that he has been taken away from his work. Obviously the conditions of growth are not in situations such as these. No mere sentimental devotion to democracy on the part of the status leader will change the situation. A way must be found to identify each member of the group with enterprise which is under way. This identification is probably facilitated by a permanent organization in which the responsibilities of members are determined democratically.

On the other hand, it is easy to find examples of groups at work on genuine problems, whose members are experienc-

[6] See "On the Symptoms and Survival of Senile Groups," by Alvin F. Zander (*Educational Leadership*, V:319–22, February, 1948).

ing continuous growth. Let a school faculty, for example, set about the task of curriculum reorganization in response to a felt need and the conditions for developing creativeness begin to emerge. The school becomes more than a collection of buildings and individuals. It takes on a dynamic character. The challenge of the situation requires all the genius which can be marshalled. The problems presented require all of the talent of the teaching staff. Some members will be involved in research, others in writing, still others in experimental teaching. New organizations grow out of a need to solve a problem or to meet a new situation. New leaders will arise out of the staff under the challenge of the new situation. In this way is achieved "the development of each, through the cooperation of all." [7]

6. *The status leader facilitates the process by means of which decisions on common problems are reached.*

The preceding discussion of the principle involved in the group process have of necessity dealt with the role of the status leader, who in a college or university would likely be the president, the dean, a department head, the chairman of a committee, or the teacher in the classroom. The purpose of the present discussion is to focus upon the problem of defining more precisely the manner in which the status leader functions in the democratic group process.

As has been pointed out earlier, we are prone to divide people into two classes, leaders and followers. We spend much time discussing how we may somehow separate this "leader" group of young people from the "follower" group in order to give them more attention and thus prepare them for their ultimate roles of leadership in our society. In the high school we get them to elect Latin instead of home economics on the ground that they will be better prepared

[7] *Group Planning in Education,* by Harry H. Giles, p. 143 (Washington: Department of Supervision and Curriculum Development of N. E. A., 1945).

for college which is the next higher level of education for leadership. Another favorite scheme employed by the college for selecting the "leaders" is to accept only the "upper seventh" or "upper third" of the graduating class. Those who are not accepted presumably are the "followers." It seems fairly evident that, as our society is now organized, the so-called followers are going to have more and more responsibility for determining national policy. The so-called "élite" may be rudely pushed aside. It seems only good sense that we give attention to the education of all for a citizenship that demands increasing ability to use the method of intelligence in making decisions. This is only saying that in a democracy all men are in a certain sense regarded as leaders. The traditional theory of leadership has been aptly described as *leadership by an élite* by Alice Miel, which "is based upon the premise that the majority of people are not wise enough to govern themselves; they are born to be followers. Only a chosen few, the élite, are gifted with powers of leadership." [8]

Many public school and college administrations subscribe to and practice this theory. The speak of *my* school, *my* department, *my* college, *my* teaching staff. They hand down the policies to be followed and demand "cooperation" from their followers. Their leadership derives from the legal powers vested in them, rather than from the contributions which they may make in a democratic group. Traditionally, supervisors have held to the theory also and have assumed superior knowledge and judgment. They were busy writing courses of studies, issuing directives to the teachers, checking lesson plans, and observing and evaluating the teacher—often by the use of some rating which passed judgment on the teacher's personality, knowledge of the subject, "discipline," and the like. Is it any wonder that teachers have as a class shown so little creativeness?

[8] Alice Miel, *op. cit.*, pp. 149–150.

Fortunately, under the impact of a gradual process of democratization which has been developing for some time, and the numerous studies of human motivation[9] and behavior, a new concept of leadership is developing which refuses to make clear-cut divisions between leaders and followers but which regards all people as having potentialities for leadership if the conditions for functioning are maintained.[10] It is out of this background that has evolved the conception of *status leader* which has been implied in the above discussion. It remains to make it more explicit.

The status leader helps the group to define its goal and to plan ways of realizing them. In short, he is an expert in the group process and helps the group to use it effectively. In some cases he may have to take drastic measures to protect the process.

The status leader helps the group to discover the most effective ways of working, the appropriate use of special abilities of members, and ways of discovering their hidden talents.

The status leader helps the group to provide the appropriate physical conditions for effective work. Many a committee bogs down because it has no stenographic service, no appropriate place to meet, or because the work has to be done in *addition* to a staggering load of other duties which must be carried on.

The status leader contributes to the on-going process in terms of his own special competencies. This is merely another way of saying that his contributions are to be made and evalu-

[9] *The Social Problems of an Industrial Civilization*, by Elton Mayo (Cambridge: Harvard University Press, 1945).

[10] For example, see "Experiments in Leadership Training," by Leslie Zelemy (*Journal of Educational Sociology*, XIV, January, 1941, pp. 310–13), and "Training in Democratic Leadership," by Alex Bavelor and Kurt Lewin (*Journal of Abnormal and Social Psychology*, XXXVII, January, 1942, pp. 115–19).

ated by precisely the same standards as those of other members. His ideas have no priority simply on the grounds of his having some *"official"* *status*.

The status leader has a special responsibility in improving group morale, helping members to find security and status, in giving encouragement for work well done, and for the general improvement of human relations within the group.

The status leader serves as a coordinator of the activities of the group. As such he aids in making plans and in providing whatever structuring is needed to keep the enterprise moving toward the goals to which the group is committed.

To those who are in the habit of thinking in terms of the "leadership of the élite," the role of the leader stated herein may seem somewhat trivial. It may seem lacking in the dynamic quality so frequently sought by boards of trustees when they select administrators. It is not easy to shift one's thinking from the conception of the dynamics of the situation springing from a gifted leader to the conception of the dynamics of the group. Those who have experienced the satisfaction of the latter concept, however, will testify to its effectiveness. If educational institutions practiced group dynamics techniques more effectively there would be fewer promising education programs that die when the leader moves on to other fields of endeavor. A study of the reasons why so many educational reforms fail will reveal that they were not grounded solidly in the democratic process. They were directed by authoritarians who had the power to force obedience to their wills, or by "inspiring" leaders who, by the sheer force of personality, succeeded in having others accept their ideas. Educational reforms which take place as the result of the democratic group process may be brilliantly conceived and they may also stand the test of survival.

PART TWO
Practices in the Administration
of Higher Education

CHAPTER VI

PRACTICES IN DETERMINING INSTITUTIONAL OBJECTIVES

HAROLD C. HAND

University of Illinois

ANYTHING, whether formalized or not, that a college or university, in any of its parts and through any of its staff or student personnel while under its control, tries to do in the name of the institution in question is to be regarded as an institutional objective.

A one-man appraisal based on this definition of institutional objectives cannot be expected to yield quantified data definitive of the number of colleges and universities that typify this or that practice. There are two principal reasons for this assertion. For one thing, the usual survey techniques—whether through interviews or by questionnaire—would be inadequate in the extreme for, as thus defined, the objectives of any given institution would be but partially known by any person or body of persons who could conveniently be queried. Secondly, even fewer—probably not more than a small minority—of the institution's objectives as thus viewed would be anywhere a matter of written record. Even the combining of the two approaches could be expected to yield but a partial picture of the institutional objectives which actually obtain on whatever the campus.

This chapter, however, attempts to enumerate the principal ways in which colleges and universities through their staffs and students try to do things in the name of the institution. Mainly, then, whatever value this chapter may afford the reader will consist in suggesting a point of view, illuminated by occasional illustrations, which he may find it profitable to utilize in appraising his own institution.

A FRAME OF REFERENCE

Before we begin our attempt to describe, we should make clear the simple frame of reference from which we derive the benchmarks we shall utilize in appraising the practices to be noted. One of the basic postulates of democracy is that all who are to be affected by the operation of a policy (objective) should be consulted in reference to, and have a part in shaping, that policy. If, because of the size of the group or for whatever other adequate reason, this consultation must be carried on through representatives, these representatives should be chosen by the group in question. We also take it to be a basic postulate of democracy that at any given moment the will of the majority shall obtain, but that all minorities shall be free to utilize the democratic processes of free discussion in their attempts to change a minority into a majority point of view. Pending such persuasion, the minority is obligated to "go along" with the majority and not employ obstructionist tactics. It is also a postulate of democracy that there be respect for and obedience to legally constituted authority, provided only that said authority is operating within its authorized sphere. As applied to colleges and universities, this last means among other things that the broad purposes for which each is chartered define the charter of freedom within the institution. No objective contrary to these purposes may legitimately be advanced by any member of the college community.

THE FORMULATION OF OBJECTIVES

We have already mentioned what is perhaps the most basic general determinant of institutional objectives; namely, the enabling acts passed or the charters granted by legislative or other legal bodies. These documents indicate the broad purpose or purposes within which the institutions are authorized to operate. Although ordinarily couched in general terms, they always imply broad limits to the objectives beyond which the institutions in question may not legitimately attempt to operate.

The regents or trustees thus brought into being or authorized constitute the bodies which alone are legally empowered to legislate the operational policies of the institutions over which they preside. These bodies almost invariably formulate and commonly publish statutes (by whatever name) embodying these operational policies. This document becomes the "constitution" for the college or university in question, and so long as it retains its legal sanction is subject to amendment only on the part of the regents or trustees themselves. Commonly, however, these amendments are initiated by recommendations transmitted by the president of the college or university in question. These recommendations, in turn, frequently originate with the staff and in some instances with the student body of the institution. All recommendations looking to policies which promise to affect the work or well-being of either the staff or the student body should be considered by the group to be affected, and their funded opinions solicited and given weight in the final recommendation. This is not uncommonly done, with varying degrees of thoroughness and sincerity, in reference to the academic staff. Unless it is strongly organized, the nonacademic staff is much less frequently thus brought into the participatory process. Even less frequently are the student bodies to be affected so consulted and involved.

Our institutions of higher learning, in concert with the lower schools, are supposed to be laboratories of democracy in which the democratic way of life is learned through living democratically as well as through formal instruction. In addition, it is to our college and university-trained men and women that our communities should be able to look with confidence for leaders. Central among the types of leadership which should thus be provided by the institutions of higher learning is leadership in reference to the democratic way of life itself, not just the narrowly conceived leaderships variously peculiar to the several professions. Colleges and universities in which students are excluded from the participatory process not only are failing to utilize a potentially fruitful laboratory opportunity, but they are also derelict in their duty inasmuch as training in the democratic process is the right of every student in our society. Teachers who are not themselves living democratically can scarcely be expected to be maximally effective in engendering the attitudes and skills appropriate to a democracy. To deny the participation of the faculty in policy matters is to impoverish our curriculum. In like vein, students in institutions in which the nonacademic staff is treated in a cavalier manner can scarcely be expected to believe that the college is sencerely devoted to the principles of democracy. Democracy is unlikely to be nurtured in an undemocratic environment.

This mention of the part students should have in the determining of institutional purposes suggest the desirability of noting some of the important roles they typically play in this regard, usually unwittingly and too frequently undemocratically. Since institutional objectives are embodied in what "goes on" in all on-campus living groups and other extra-class activities, it follows that these should be scrutinized for the determinants which are operative therein.

In these groups and activities there is usually more rather than less actual student self-government. Since every experience leaves one to some degree a changed person, and since the student leaders play an important part in determining what these experiences are to be, it follows that they constitute a very real force in determining the institutional objectives here connoted. An illustration may prove helpful at this point.

SOME LABORATORY EXERCISES

If the campus is to be a laboratory in which students acquire greater proficiency in the skills of democratic living through actually living democratically, the institutional objectives striven for through living groups and all other extra-class activities would include the engendering in each student of the feeling that he "belongs," that he is "wanted," that he "counts" for something, and that he has a legitimate "place in the sun." These objectives would also include the combatting of cliques and snobbery, the breaking down of racial and religious prejudices, the inducing of respect for the sacredness of human personality, and many others validly derived from the postulates of democracy.

In living groups and other extra-class activities from which students of whatever religion, skin color, and/or economic status (to name but three factors which are too commonly operative) are excluded, the experiences thus provided are obviously antidemocratic in character. Whether recognized or not, and whether approved by the college authorities or not, the institutional objectives here operative are the very opposites of those noted in the preceding paragraph. If, as frequently happens, the student leaders sanction, encourage, or enforce these exclusions, they are playing a decisive role in determining institutional objectives directly antithetical to those which should obtain. If, however, these leaders resist and ultimately remedy these undemocratic practices, they are likewise functioning in the determination of institutional objectives, but desirably so. This lesson should be effectively taught not only to all student leaders but to the entire student body and to the faculty. Few institutions of higher learning make any systematic provision for so doing. Only in scattered instances is there an adequate awareness of the fact that extra-class activities constitute an informal but potent curriculum, and that institutional objectives operate here as well as in the formal courses.

Faculty Role in Policy-Making

With this digression completed, let us return to our consideration of the ways in which institutional objectives are formally determined. The statutes of the Board of Regents (by whatever title either is known) generally lodge certain responsibilities and their correlative powers in the faculty senate (however titled). These invariably have to do with the internal policies (objectives) of the institution and their administration. Too frequently, membership in this body is restricted by statute or by-law to faculty persons in the upper ranks, and seldom indeed is student representation permitted, much less encouraged. Since this body is almost continuously concerning itself with policies (objectives) which affect the total faculty and the total student body, often in vital ways, it follows that no institution in which these exclusions are practiced can legitimately contend that it is operating in a thoroughly democratic manner. Hence it cannot validly assert that it is maximally dedicated to the engendering of the democratic way of life. The exclusions just noted typify a species of paternalism antithetical to democracy. The lower faculty ranks as well as the student body should be represented.

It is at the departmental or school or college level that the most intimate, and not infrequently the most significant, policy considerations are treated and translated into program. Here, too, paternalism is too frequently the rule. In the larger institutions particularly there is often a policy committee in the department, school, or college. If democracy is being practiced in a thorough-going manner by the department, school, or college, membership on this policy committee will be representative of all faculty ranks and of the student body in question. Furthermore, these representatives will be selected by the faculty and by the students, not hand-picked by the department head or dean. Far too frequently, however, only faculty persons in the upper ranks are entitled to serve. Regrettably, students are but seldom represented.

In too many situations a "strong" (à la Hitler) dean or department head makes the policy decisions himself without benefit of consultation with either the faculty or the student body. From the democratic point of view, this is "efficiency" in college administration at its dictatorial worst. Not infrequently, however, this is as much the fault of the faculty as of the dean or department head. Some faculty members, unfortunately, are not willing to discharge the responsibilities which democratic participation in college administration necessarily entails. Others appear to feel more comfortable when they are "told" what to do. By definition, neither type of staff person is competent to teach in the schools of a democracy.

PERSONNEL POLICIES

The objects to be striven for are also set to an undetermined but probably appreciable degree by the policy of the department, school, or college in reference to promotions in rank and pay. What is rewarded tends to get done, what goes unrewarded tends to be neglected. Hence, whoever determines promotion policy in a real sense determines objectives.

Far too frquently for the good health of democracy, deans and department heads regard the making of promotion policy as their special and exclusive prerogative. Only slightly less undesirable from the democratic point of view is the practice of sharing this responsibility with the senior professors. Since the total staff is both immediately and importantly affected, it is clear that the full faculty group concerned should participate—through representatives of their own choosing, if the faculty is too large to function as a committee of the whole—in the defining of promotion policies.

Despite the fact that it is they who are ultimately the most affected, students are all but universally excluded from participating in the formulating of policies governing promotion. Obviously, they should not only be privileged but expected so to participate.

Since policies almost invariably get remade as they are administered, it is clear that whoever administers the promotion policy also determines objectives. Few, indeed, are the situations in which this important aspect of administration is in the hands of anyone but the dean or department head or in those of this functionary and a small handful of the senior staff members. Almost nonexistent are the situations in which the students have any systematically provided for part in this process. Since both groups are affected, both the faculty and the students should participate in the administering as well as the formulating of promotion policies.

Closely allied to, and fully as important as, promotion policies in determining institutional objectives are the policies and practices which govern the selection of new staff personnel. Over the long haul, what one wants to and is able to do will in major part determine what objects of action or feeling he will strive for; especially is this likely to be true in the relatively free and almost completely unsupervised situations in which most college and university instructors operate. The question of "who" is employed, i.e., what he values and what his convictions and abilities are, is thus one which should be resolved on the basis of general faculty and representative student participation. Too often, deans or department heads make these decisions too much on their own, with consultation restricted to no more than a few senior staff members. Again, students are almost never involved in any way in shaping this subtle but very real determinant of institutional objectives.

BUDGET POLICIES

The budget is still another basic determinant of institutional objectives, and a potent one. Deans and department heads who constitute themselves a committee of one for purposes of shaping and administering the budget thus assume a one-man dictation of what the objectives are in major part to be. From the democratic standpoint, it is only slightly less undesirable to extend this paternalism to include the senior ranks. Since all are to be affected, all should be included in the participatory process. This appears to have been done commendably in a considerable number of situations. Rare, however, is the institution in which the students' proper concern with the budget is permitted direct expression in any systematic way.

A special case of the budget as a determinant of objectives is afforded by the grants successfully solicited from foundations and other benefactors. The decisions as to the purposes for which such funds are to be sought are too commonly made by but one or a few staff members. Since the character of what is to be striven for by the department, school, or college is invariably affected by grants of any appreciable magnitude, it follows that the decision as to what projects are to be promoted should be as broadly based as any other policy which is determinative of institutional objectives.

In our consideration of the various internal ways in which institutional objectives are determined, we have consistently argued that the full faculty and the student body should be represented. We have also implied that the nonacademic staff should be consulted regarding matters of concern to its members. The machinery for providing full faculty representation has long since been invented and has for so many years been employed in so many institutions that no further mention of it seems necessary here. Only in scattered instances, however, have ways been found to bring representatives of the students and of the nonacademic staff to the council table. How these representatives can best be secured will of course vary from campus to campus. At one midwestern institution, student representatives to the top-ranking policy committee are selected by the Student Council. At another, those who represent the students both in this policy and in all meetings of the full faculty are named by an organization (open to all students) known as the Student Forum. Although it is anathema to many presidents and deans, the labor union appears to offer what is perhaps the most satisfactory way of providing that the voice of the nonacademic staff will be heard in reference to policies affecting its members' work or welfare.

"Outside" Policy-Making Agencies

This takes us into a consideration of "outside" budgetary influences. No informed person denies that the great foundations have profoundly affected the character of institutional objectives in many of the colleges and universities of America over the past few decades. In a real sense, those who have controlled the policies of these foundations have by this fact materially shaped the policies of the institutions of higher learning in this country.

Industrial concerns represent another outside determinant of institutional objectives. With generous funds allocated in support of a whole host of research projects in which they are interested, many of these organizations have contracted with many of our institutions of higher learning for the prosecution of these researches. These contracts not infrequently require that the institution embark upon types of research little if at all related to its central purposes—pursuits in which it would never engage were it not for the lure of this outside money. Further, when the project is at an end, the institution not infrequently finds itself encumbered with added staff members who are either out of sympathy with or incapable of doing (or both) the type of research dictated by the central purposes of the university. Unless it can maintain its own integrity in so doing, it seems extremely unwise for a college or university to accept—much less solicit—these outside research grants from industry or business.

Much the same comment must be made regarding research contracts offered by governmental agencies, for all of the observations just noted apply. Added to this is the further fact that many of the governmental contracts are associated with one or the other of the military establishments and are frequently of the "hush-hush" variety. By definition, any such "hush-hush" enterprise puts an effective stop to communication among staff members. When this happens, it can scarcely be said that the institution is maintaining its integrity.

There are numerous other outside influences which operate to determine institutional objectives. Many of these are desirable, but others cannot be sanctioned by the postulates of democracy.

Among these influences, one that is actively sought and promoted by enlightened faculties is that wielded by an advisory committee made up of people in the "field" who stand in some unique relationship to the department, school, or college in question. To illustrate, the advisory committee to the college of education in a midwestern university is variously made up of individuals representative of all groups in the state served in any direct way by this college. This advisory committee meets on the campus twice each year. It advises in reference to the educational needs of the commonwealth and recommends curriculum and service emphases to the faculty of the college. Reciprocally, new policies contemplated by the college are "tried out" before this committee and its advice as to their desirability sought. Material improvements in the institutional objectives of this college of education have resulted from this particular outside influence.

Another kind of desirable outside influence is manifest through the work of the various civic improvement, social welfare, and like agencies which are commonly found in American life. These organizations serve to heighten the sensitivity of college and university faculties to meet educational needs and thus exercise an indirect but very appreciable effect on the determining of institutional objectives.

Those legislators and donors who are affectionately known to the profession as "the friends of education" constitute a third type of desirable outside influence. The funds they legislate or give make possible the achieving of new institutional objectives as well as the strengthening of those already operative.

Other self-styled friends of education are frequently a hindrance rather than a help. Included here is the eccentric donor who dangles a tempting sum before the harassed president which is his if he will build this or that building, establish this or that chair, or otherwise perpetuate the donor's "fame." Too often, nothing is tendered to pay for the maintenance or upkeep of the building, so the net result promises to be imbalance if not impoverishment; yet the president hesitates to decline the offer lest it be bruited about that his institution is not receptive to donations. The proposed chair is not infrequently in the service of some objective which is at best but peripheral to the central purposes of the college. Again, however, the president hesitates to discourage the would-be donor for fear of jeopardizing his other sources of endowment. In these ways, institutional objectives are not uncommonly modified. There is still another species of self-styled friends of education typified by the American Council *for* Education (not to be confused with the American Council *on* Education). These "friends" are in fact enemies of democratic education, for they spread unfounded charges that the public schools are subversive. In essence, they are propaganda agencies dedicated to maintaining the *status quo*. If they prove successful in doing what they have set out to do, institutional objectives will have been radically changed by outside agencies whose premises regarding both education and democracy are sharply at variance with those of Thomas Jefferson.

The findings and recommendations of influential commissions, committees, or other groups concerned with higher education and its problems make up another kind of outside influence which, if their recommendations be critically appraised and adapted to the local situation, must usually be regarded as desirable. Relatively recent conspicuous illustrations are the Report of the President's Commission on Higher Education, the work of the Harvard Committee reported in *General Education in a Free Society*, and the work of a group at the University of Iowa entitled *Toward General Education*. These pronouncements are invariably based on a more or less thorough-going analysis of the job to be done through higher education. They describe or imply the qualities of the person adequately equipped through education to live effectively in today's world and, so far as it can be foreseen, in the world of tomorrow. The recommendations of the report are then derived from what the authors think it takes, programatically speaking, to produce the desired sort of person. This general method is one that is frequently utilized by departments, schools, and colleges in the determining of institutional objectives.

Although it may not be correct to designate them as outside influences, the various national and regional professional organizations in which college and university presidents, deans, and professors hold membership also generally exert a creditable influence in the determining of institutional objectives. Of these, one of the most influential is probably the American Association of University Professors.

Although the provisions they severely enforce may at times be a hindrance to rather than an aid for the changes which are necessary in a rapidly changing world, the various "accrediting" agencies which either grant or withhold recognition must usually be chalked up on the credit side of the ledger as still another outside influence on the determining of institutional objectives. Much of the same comment is warranted in reference to the licensing boards whose business it is to scrutinize the qualifications of various of the professional schools and colleges. The five-year "moratorium" recently declared by the Land Grant colleges wholesomely reminds us that our institutions of higher learning can be expected to "balk" when the requirements of accrediting agencies become hurtful. Reference here is to the practice of asking, in effect, "What is being done at such and such prestige-bearing institutions?" and then modeling as closely as possible after the pattern or patterns thus revealed. This "monkey-cage" method may have something to recommend it, but the present writer regards it as an extremely dubious procedure.

No recital of outside influences on the determining of institutional objectives would be complete without mention of the alumni. The potency of this force is attested by numerous stadia extending from Yale to Stanford and from Minnesota to Texas. In the shadows of these colossal structures live professors of chemistry, English, and mathematics whose salaries are but a fraction of those paid to the men who preside over the athletic activities of the institution.

This brings us to legislative enactments and investigations as an outside influence on the determining of institutional objectives. With but a scattered few exceptions, these enactments and investigations are undesirable in their institutional consequences. Too frequently, the enacting and the investigating are done by persons with little or no conception of what the purposes of an institution of higher learning should be, and with even less knowledge of how these can best be accomplished. At worst, these acts are performed by bigots with a perverted view not only of higher education but of democracy itself. Significantly, these legislative hindrances are most commonly perpetrated in periods of national hysteria when, by definition, men are prone to take leave of their senses. As these lines were written (1950) it is all too apparent that many legislators are again the captives of such a hysteria.

Pressure groups constitute another source of outside influence which is almost without exception undesirable. These groups range widely over virtually every conceivable interest—antivivesection, isolationism, world federalism, rugged individualism, the welfare state, and so on and on. All that most have in common is that each wants its particular and invariably partial version of truth taught as *the* truth in the schools and colleges. Examination of their premises is usually regarded as an attack on the foundations of the social order by these would-be determiners of institutional objectives. Vaguely phrased oath laws and the censoring of textbooks constitute the tools to which the more reactionary of these groups almost instinctively turn in order to pervert education to their particular pattern. How far this perversion threatens to go in the present period of hysteria is darkly foreshadowed by the number of such oath laws now on the statute books and by the action of the Un-American Activities Committee in calling on over a hundred colleges to submit a full list of their textbooks for investigation.

Conclusion

Although a sizeable number and variety of ways in which institutional objectives are determined have been discussed in this chapter, the full enumeration has by no means been completed. Enough have probably been instanced, however, to demonstrate the fruitfulness of the definition on which this section of the book was based. With the illustrations given, it is believed that the reader can readily utilize this definition in ferreting out for himself the multiform influences which shape the determining of the objectives of his particular institution.

CHAPTER VII

PRACTICES IN DETERMINING INSTRUCTIONAL ACTIVITIES

HARVEY H. DAVIS

State University of Iowa

INSTRUCTIONAL activities are properly designed in the most forward-looking colleges and universities to achieve educational objectives when they have been developed along the lines set forth in Part III of this *Yearbook*. It is true that some have failed to carry through fully from the blueprint stage of stated objectives to the actual construction stage in building programs. It is also true that some institutions use the objectives as window dressing, or merely to meet accrediting requirements, but in general a serious effort is made to devise instructional activities with a view to meeting objectives.

THE FACULTY'S PLACE IN CARRYING OUT OBJECTIVES

Accrediting associations are more and more disposed to base evaluation of institutions upon the way they serve their constituencies rather than upon a rigid tabulation of degrees held, books in libraries, and square feet of floor space. The North Central Association of Secondary Schools and Colleges makes clear in its statement of standards the need for a statement of purposes which are regarded as a guide in determining the policies and activities of the institution. The Association also emphasizes the importance of faculty participation and student understanding in the creation of these purposes. The pronouncement goes on to point out that unless the curriculum and modes of instruction are influenced by the statement of purposes the statement cannot be regarded as operative.

The actual instructional procedures in the classroom are in terms of the objectives when the faculty understands the objectives and is in reasonably close agreement with them. If this is not the case, the instructors will tend to teach toward their own objectives no matter what the catalog says, and no matter what the other published reports from the institution may indicate. The wise administration, therefore, which is genuinely eager to make its institution function in meeting the needs of youth and society, makes sure that the faculty participates fully in preparing every stage of the statement of objectives. Even after the statement has been made in this manner, the best practice is to make provision to familiarize every faculty member with the statement and its implications. This is particularly necessary in view of the fact that rapid turnover of staff results in the early addition of many faculty members who have not had a chance to participate in the initial statement of objectives.

Implementing Objectives

At the Fourth National Conference on Higher Education of the National Education Association, one group emphasized the fact that general education is a philosophy, a spirit, and an ideal rather than a mere group of courses or pattern of integrated courses. They went on to stress the importance of making the faculty aware of this spirit and engaging them in participating in this ideal and philosophy. What is true of general education is equally true of the practices necessary to achieve objectives in the rest of the higher education program. The relative newness of general education as a specific part of the college program may even make it easier to achieve this faculty spirit among those who are dealing directly with that program than is the case in older programs where vested interests have become more deeply intrenched.

In developing a plan for instructional activities from the necessarily rather general statement of objectives for the institution as a whole, it becomes essential to divide the task among the units of the institution. In the interest of efficiency and economy, each unit does what it is best prepared to do and duplication of activities between colleges, departments, or other divisions is kept at a minimum. It follows, therefore, that each college is responsible for making its own set of objectives in general conformity with the institutional statement, again emphasizing faculty participation. This is done by college faculty committees working closely with the institutional committee. The college statements are naturally more specific than the institutional one, and can be directed toward the particular profession for which the college is preparing youth. These committees where most successful look beyond the campus to the profession for which its graduates are being prepared. A committee from a modern veterinary college faculty notes at once the relative change in importance of horses and poultry in the nation during the past twenty years, with the consequent shift in practice of doctors of veterinary medicine, and modifies its objectives accordingly. In colleges of education the statements are directed toward the preparation of teachers for elementary schools, secondary schools, administrators, or whatever groups are being served. Such modern trends as those toward the development of community colleges, wider scope of instruction in world problems and emphasis on the democratic way of government are considered carefully.

Within the college, each department or other division makes its own statement which again is in conformity with the college statement and which is more specific than that for the college as a whole. It is essential that the interpretation of the objectives be made in terms of desirable types of understanding and behavior to be developed in the students. Unless the objectives are so developed, there is danger that an interpretation will be made in terms entirely of subject matter and the learning of facts. Valuable as factual and other knowledge may be, the possession of such knowledge will not guarantee the behavior patterns toward which education must work if the final results are to be satisfied.

If an education college includes such special divisions as music or library training, appropriate statements of objectives in addition to the ones suggested for the college as a whole will naturally be in order. At the departmental level, it is not only practical but highly desirable that every faculty member participate, even though the writing of the statement which is finally to be approved is done by a committee.

PUTTING OBJECTIVES IN COURSE OFFERINGS

With a clear departmental statement of objectives thus formulated, careful examination is made of all course offerings to see that they are designed to contribute to the objectives. It is essential that the department be ruthless in deleting courses, or parts of them, which are of honored tradition, the result of personal taste of some instructor, or merely copied from some other institution, if they do not make a worthwhile contribution to the attainment of the agreed-upon objectives. It is important also that the department be continuously alert to add courses as special needs arise within the framework of the objectives, and equally alert to discard them when the need passes. Some of the courses set up for training teachers to meet special demands on the schools which grew out of the war emergency have now been removed. On the other hand, alert colleges of education are now setting up special courses or combinations of courses to prepare as well as possible some persons from the high school field to serve in meeting the serious shortage of elementary teachers.

The college, or department of education, in meeting its objectives is confronted with the necessity for providing activities so balanced as to give adequate understanding of child growth and development, the learning process, and such mastery of subject matter as is necessary to serve the particular field in which the teacher is to work. The battle between those extremists holding the view that anyone who knows his subject can teach it, and those who hold that anyone who understands children and who is skilled in method need not worry about subject matter, is less violent than it once was. Nevertheless, those who plan for the education of teachers are still aware of the existence of these points of view.

PROBLEMS OF INSTRUCTIONAL OBJECTIVES IN PROFESSIONAL COURSES

Instructional activities for the education of persons for the teaching profession go far beyond preparing them for efficient work in the classroom. There are many activities which are designed to give them an understanding of the place of the school in society, both historical and current, and the place of the school in an ordinary community. To be truly effective, the instructional activities in these areas must also emphasize the part which the prospective teacher will play in maintaining and improving the status of the school.

Professional colleges of all sorts are recognizing the importance of more general education for their students. Some are requiring more of such work in the preprofessional requirements, others are lengthening the professional curricula and mixing general education and professional education throughout. The latter believe that some general education is better secured in the later years of the curriculum when greater maturity and better motivation add to the values gained. They also believe that some professional courses can be taken much earlier than has been the custom. Some professional courses are no more difficult than general education courses and the advantages of earlier introduction to special preparation for a chosen profession are considerable. Colleges of education are often found in this group. By this practice the student is introduced to his professional preparation by appropriate stages. The transition, for example, from observation of good teaching practices to participation in them, and then to responsible practice teaching, is not violent if it can be carried out over a period of three or four years. If, on the other hand, the student attempts to cram all of his actual observation and practice into the last year or the last semester of his college course, it is much less effective and is a much less satisfactory experience. Another advantage of an earlier introduction to professional work is that it gives the student a better opportunity to make an intelligent early decision as to whether he really wants to make teaching his career and, if so, what phase of teaching is most attractive to him. A further important result of this early introduction to professional work is that the student can see clearly what the consequences of his decision to enter a particular profession are likely to be. For example, if he decides that he wants to be a teacher of mathematics, he must understand the extent of competence in that field which will be required by the curriculum which he is about to enter.

Faculty Participation in Objective Formulation

By providing for complete faculty participation in the formulation of objectives, each member is clear as to the place of his courses in the whole scale of things and can in turn make clear to his classes just what the goals of the courses and the noncourse experiences are, and the means to be used in reaching them. It goes without saying that the teacher will select the subject matter and plan student activities, both individual and group, in the manner most likely to achieve the goals. Advantages both in terms of the quality of student activity and in terms of giving the students a feeling of belonging will be gained if students are brought into the planning situation as far as possible. Certainly with respect to appropriate field trips and special types of investigation, student participation and planning can be easily effected and should be utilized to the fullest. If the purpose of the course is to develop an appreciation of literature, the activities both in the classroom and those carried on out of class by assignment will aim toward that objective with fractionating and dissection kept at a minimum. It has been demonstrated that a sophomore class in Shakespeare enrolling several hundred students can be well taught in an auditorium with proper method and equipment. Recordings from great Shakespearean actors, reading and discussion by a competent teacher, and some scenes presented by talented students are effective as is shown by the fact that more reading by the class and a better appreciation of the greatness of the man and his works are gained in this manner than by intensive study by small sections of the class in ordinary classrooms. After all, the plays were written to be presented to sizable audiences with the idea that they would enjoy and appreciate them. If the improvement of skill in written composition is the aim, then the activities of the class are designed to achieve that result. In this case, large classes are not suitable for continuous practice. Close reading of papers and numerous conferences are required.

Courses designed to give nonscience majors an understanding of the role of science in society and some appreciation of the scientific method are intended to do that rather than to be practical duplications of first courses for science majors. In the education of teachers for elementary schools, such courses are very much more satisfactory than are the ordinary elementary courses in the areas concerned. The course in food preparation for prospective home economics teachers, on the other hand, is properly designed with a view to enable the students to make progress toward ability to prepare real meals under conditions usually surrounding the preparation of such meals. To this end carefully planned and supervised practice with standard kitchen equipment is in order.

The responsibility of administrative officers—institutional, college, and departmental—in the assignment of faculty is very considerable in this connection. It is obviously important that the person in charge of the course be capable of managing the course effectively and that he be enthusiastic about doing so. Little can be hoped from courses taught in a fumbling manner or taught by instructors with tongue in cheek. This is especially important in the education of teachers because the so-called subject-matter courses taken by the prospective teacher are frequently taught by faculty members of colleges other than education. If these persons are not familiar with and sympathetic to the objectives, they may do much to confuse and discourage the student. One of the best solutions to this problem is that of having the subject-matter teachers who bear major responsibility for that phase of the education of teachers hold joint appointments in education and in their field of specialization. In filling vacancies which occur from time to time in the faculties of the various departments concerned with teacher education, extreme care is taken to select persons most exactly fitted by education, experience, and attitude to take the part in the program which the particular position carries.

The graduate schools which are responsible for preparing college teachers are increasingly aware of the need for fitting them for responsible service in the colleges to which they are to go. In the case of preparation for the education of teachers, this goes beyond the education of persons for the handling of methods courses and includes preparation of persons for subject matter fields who are sympathetic to the needs of public school teachers. Programs in some graduate colleges include internships both on and off the campus to prepare the prospective faculty member for participation in work beyond the teaching of the courses to which he is to be assigned. While graduate faculties ordinarily do not favor comparing this experience with practice teaching, it actually serves about the same purpose.

A Faculty's Experience in Meeting Objectives

Frequent attention in faculty meetings to the effectiveness of the program in meeting objectives aids in keeping all eyes on the goals and in sharing experience. Otherwise the human tendency to assume that a problem once solved will stay solved is likely to result in a static situation which by comparison means going backward. When several persons teach various sections of the same course, there is much profit in conferences on methods used by each, and reports of various successes and difficulties. Naturally, all graduate assistants and readers will participate in such conferences. The experience of the Associated Colleges of Upper New York, when the unusual opportunity of starting a new institution with no traditions and no vested interests arose, is of interest at this point:

Of special concern, of course, was the actual classroom performance of the teachers. The general scheme, as developed by all departments, embraced the following procedures:

1. Individual conferences with instructors to offer suggestions
2. Informal group conferences for sharing of ideas and comparing of notes
3. Demonstrations of marking of papers, and study of comparative charts of the marks of all teachers of the same subject on each campus and on all of the campuses
4. Encouragement of intervisitation and observation of more experienced teachers
5. Actual presentation of lesson content, in some instances, before material was presented to students
6. Training in phrasing of "quiz" questions to state clearly what the student should do in the way of synthesis, analysis, and statement of accurate information
7. Encouragement of self-evaluation.[1]

In connection with evaluation phases of the above procedures, it will be seen at once that all evaluation procedures should be in terms of the extent to which understandings and behavior patterns of the students have been developed, consistent with the objectives. In group meetings and in department meetings, discussion of the evaluation procedures and of the results is appropriate. There is also opportunity for staff to evaluate each other and some colleges are making good use of student evaluation at this point.

The importance of the tests used can hardly be overemphasized. Unless evaluative procedures are consistent with instructional practices and objectives, the whole program becomes ineffective. Students rightly or wrongly seek to make good grades and unless the evaluative measures on which grades are based are well designed to indicate the degree of success in meeting the objectives which have been stated for the course, they do their work with an eye to the tests rather than to the presumed objectives.

[1] "In-Service Education of the College Faculty," by Amy M. Gilbert, in *The Journal of Higher Education* (20:4:195, April, 1949).

Some Administrative Contributions

The administration is also responsible for providing classrooms and laboratories designed and equipped in such a way as to facilitate instructional activities in line with the objectives. If student participation and discussion is essential to the instructional activities, then the classroom must make this easy and natural. Rows of fixed seats all oriented toward the instructor tempt him to lecture rather than to develop class discussion and exchange of opinion. Laboratories when properly designed are constructed and equipped so as to aid and encourage the various instructional activities appropriate to progress toward particular objectives. For advanced students preparing for research careers, the apparatus for original research is provided. For students in introductory courses leading toward a major in a given field, equipment designed to develop skill in techniques is proper and in fact essential. For nonmajors, however, demonstration equipment so designed as to admit of easy observation from all parts of the room is more appropriate for some aspects of the course. The apparatus to be used by the student in such a course is designed for simple experiments illustrating basic science procedures rather than the development of skill in handling instruments. Busses to serve field trips in various areas such as geology, soil conservation, housing, and the like are essential to a broad program for the education of teachers. Teachers of modern schools need to be sensitized to current problems in relations, in housing, in public health, in industrial conditions, in conservation of natural resources, and many others.

Planned observation of conditions in real life situations is an integral part of the sensitizing process. Libraries built and equipped to integrate instruction with source materials of all sorts and to make the instructor easily available to the library situation through provision of work rooms and faculty offices in the library building are helpful. The best results in the design of libraries recently constructed, some of them of the modular type, have been achieved when liberal use has been made of faculty committees in the planning stages. Not only have better buildings been built but because of the wide faculty participation at this stage, a more immediate and intelligent use of the building has followed. Museums, art galleries, and auditoriums, all constructed with a view to actual and continuous use by the instructional program rather than merely points for sightseeing visits, are an integral part of the modern teacher preparation program. Abundant visual and auditory aids with convenient facilities for use in classrooms, laboratories, and auditoriums are also provided.

In the education of youth for the teaching profession, a demonstration school for the college of education is essential. Here the most modern methods can be observed and to some extent practiced by the students. Since very few beginning teachers will work in such schools, however, it is necessary that provision be made for observation, participation, and practice teaching in schools of various sizes in various communities and that facilities including transportation be made conveniently available. Libraries of visual and auditory aids to teaching in elementary and secondary schools are maintained for the use in practice situations by student teachers.

Throughout the whole of good relationship of the administration to instructional activities a truly democratic spirit prevails. This goes far beyond form and statement to permeate all operations and daily contacts. Promotions and salary increases are given for good teaching as readily as for evidence of the oft-mentioned "productivity" in research and writing. The administration does not stop with giving lip service to good instructional practices but follows through with tangible rewards in money and various forms of recognition for those who bring the objectives of the institution to fruition.

CHAPTER VIII

SOME PRACTICES
IN FACULTY ORGANIZATION

CLAUDE EGGERTSEN

University of Michigan

A T THE close of a recent college faculty meeting an interested observer was heard to remark that the presiding officer was the best he had ever seen. "Why, even though nearly everyone wanted to vote on that motion, the chairman prevented action!"

This attitude is the opposite of that which is desirable in the solution of college problems. It is a denial of the desirability of free intelligence and cooperation in the making of decisions by the faculty as presented in Chapters IV and V. It is a repudiation of the basic tenet that only when teachers can have confidence in group processes and can engage in conferences where there is mutual respect for differences, on the part of the leader as well as on the part of the participants, can higher education be a laboratory for democratic living.

The Commander Issues Orders

It is true that the practice of announcing the decisions of administrative officials which faculties have never discussed is an old and honored one. Faculties in American colleges have not usually had control of the institutions in which they taught. Almost from the time of the establishment of the first colonial colleges, that unique American creation, the lay governing board has assumed the responsibility of administering college affairs. It seems clear that the corporate form of organization which has been so significant in the industrial growth of the United States has been utilized in American higher education to support the concept of trustees as employers and of college teachers as employees who take direction without question.

Perhaps partly because they knew that from medieval times the faculties of European universities have enjoyed a great deal of autonomy, American college teachers, particularly in the twentieth century, have attempted to win the right to be consulted on decisions concerning educational policy. The extent to which this effort has succeeded may be discovered in part through a study of prerogatives extended to faculties in a group of colleges in a middle western region.

Practices in Selected Institutions

To administrators and faculty members of eight higher institutions, large and small, public and private, the question was asked, "What opportunities do you give prospective citizens and teachers to observe democratic practices in the administration of your institution?" For the most part, the answers were disappointing. They ranged from the candid reply that students were given none at all to the claim that, since faculty members exercised considerable control over institutional policies, students did gain from their environment some profitable experiences in shared policy-making. A number of replies were to the effect that only in supervised teaching was there a chance for college students to observe pupils, teachers, and administrators as they shared in planning and action.

Representatives of the private institution which seems to administer its affairs least in harmony with the principles presented in the early chapters of this *Yearbook* asserted that the administrative responsibility is completely that of a president who is not even accountable to a board of trustees. The powers extended to deans are granted solely at the pleasure of the president, to be taken away when and as he wills. The dean who delegates certain responsibilities and duties to faculties also does so at his wish. Faculty meetings are seldom held in the colleges of the institution. There is no academic senate or university council. In this school, therefore, students are able to observe autocracy, albeit somewhat benevolent, rather than democracy, in action in the conduct of university affairs.

Oral and written reports from two small, church-related arts colleges indicate that faculty members exercise considerable autonomy. It is true for these schools, as for every one of the eight institutions except the one described in the above paragraph, that the board of trustees is recognized to have final authority over virtually every phase of activity. In these small colleges, however, students might easily know of regular faculty meetings in which the merits of projects in which they are interested are debated. They often come into contact with committees of the faculty, to which for the most part the members are self-assigned. These committees are concerned with admissions, academic standards, athletics, class attendance, scholarships, and social activities. They act with faculty members on the boards of the student confederation and of the student union. Recently at one of these schools, students successfully insisted that the proportion of faculty members on such boards must be reduced.

It was this situation which led one faculty member to remark that the college teaching staff resembled the middle class in that it was being squeezed from two sides. Administrators are often successful in guarding their power, or even in extending it, while, at the same time, a more active and mature student population is demanding that the regulation of student affairs be taken from the faculty and that the students be allowed to evaluate the work of the teacher. This has meant in some instances that when the administrator has relinquished part of his control over salaries and promotions, students, rather than the faculty, have gained new power. This is particularly irksome to teachers in schools in which no official information about promotion policies or salary scales is made available to them.

The public institution of the eight studied which makes no claim that it follows practices in harmony with the principles advocated above has no constitution or by-laws of which copies are available for study. Through the president, powers are granted to deans and department heads rather than to the faculties of units. The chief opportunity for learning about decisions of policy occurs at the regular meetings of the "staff," to which all teachers belong. Formal decisions are made at "faculty" meetings open only to professors and associate professors and administrative personnel. It is true that many departments and some colleges in this institution accord their members as wide opportunities to act as governing bodies as faculties receive in any institution, but the right so to act is not clearly given them. Although they may have the privilege they do not have the right to be consulted about salaries and promotions. The attempts which are being made in at least one unit of the university to create a faculty-student committee on academic and social affairs are not authorized in a constitution.

Although in one college, principally engaged in the education of teachers, the faculty tried for a number of years to gain the right to participate in the making of certain administrative decisions, no real staff meeting was held there in more than a decade. The board of trustees refused to approve the constitution presented to it by representatives of the teaching body which for so long had had virtually no voice in any of the affairs of the school. A request of the faculty that it be consulted in the selection of a president was also denied, but the new executive accepted the organization proposed by the faculty as soon as he began his term. The improvement in morale, the wider participation in committee activity, and the increased attendance at faculty meetings which came as a result might as easily be noted by students in the school as it is by colleagues in nearby institutions.

The provisions of this new constitution offer so many more opportunities for faculty participation than had been true under the immediately preceding regime, and are, indeed, so much more favorable to the staff than those to be found in many colleges that they are worthy of summary. First, although it is true that the organization is advisory to the president, who must report in turn to the board in control of the college, the president himself has written, "To make it function properly it is obvious that in at least 99 cases out of 100 the president is required to follow the recommendations of the faculty."

The general faculty, composed of all resident members of the instructional and administrative staff, is constituted as a legislative body concerned with all matters of general welfare. Standing and special committees are to be elected by secret ballot. A faculty council composed of twelve elected and two *ex-officio* members is awarded broad policy-making powers concerned with any matter affecting the welfare of the college. It is instructed to act as the executive organ of the general faculty in all matters of instructional or administrative personnel. Each division of the general faculty has the obligation to make recommendations to the council on all matters which concern that division.

This institution, as well as two public ones and a private college to be discused below, adheres more closely to desirable standards of democratic administration than the one public and two private colleges briefly described above. The two public institutions, for example, possess detailed constitutions and by-laws which provide for faculty participation in the affairs of the whole institution as well as for faculty control of individual colleges. The constitution of higher public institution "A" provides that every staff member of professional rank is a voting member of the university legislature which is empowered "to consider any subject pertaining to the interests of the university and to make recommendations to the board," while "B" has established a representative university congress to have "general legislative authority over all matters concerning the university as a whole." In one of these institutions students had the opportunity to observe the faculty assert its prerogatives when students requested, gained, and publicized the aid of the faculty legislature in the removal of a speaker's ban.

In both public institutions it is the provision for faculty control of policy in the teaching units that is thought to give teachers the feelings of security and worth so essential to high morale and performance and which leads to the use of the resources of the faculty in the solution of institutional problems. The faculty of the largest college at "A," for example, assigns many of its members to important committee tasks which are related to the recognized obligation of the faculty "to provide suitable instruction and to determine the conduct of examinations, the schedule of studies, the requirements for admission and graduation."

By far the most influential committee in the largest college at "A" is the planning committee which, rather than the dean, is charged with the duty of investigating and formulating educational and instructional policies for consideration by the faculty and of acting for the college in matters related to the budget, promotions, and appointments. The full meaning of the latter part of this provision is to be seen only when it is taken in conjunction with a ruling of the trustees that "members of the professorial staff shall be appointed by the trustees on recommendation of the chairman of the department concerned and the appropriate dean, director, or executive committee, and by the president."

This committee enables the faculty to participate, through a representative group of its members, in the central administration of a large college. A rotating but permanent committee scrutinizes every important measure. Everything is done in the open and it is hoped that tendencies toward favoritism are thus eliminated. The faculty seem to remember a former period in which the dean acted as the only check upon important decisions, decisions which were sometimes made without any general knowledge of the fact until after official announcements of completed actions were made.

The same grants of power have not been given to all of the dozen other colleges in the institution. In some, membership in the faculty or in executive committees is limited to members in upper ranks, and the executive function in others is to be performed by a dean rather than a dean and a committee. In one of the colleges at "A," which has in the past few years changed its executive committee from one composed of department heads appointed by the dean to one in which members are elected by the faculty, other trends which increase the opportunities for participation of faculty members may be found. A recent revision of the by-laws provides for the choice of a chairman by committee members rather than by the dean. Where, formerly, the right to vote was enjoyed only by those of professorial rank, unless the faculty voted to give an individual instructor the right, full-time teachers were recently given the suffrage on all matters pertaining to the undergraduate program.

In a comparable college at "B," very recent changes in the constitution of the faculty seem to be closely in harmony with the principles this *Yearbook* supports. The constitution of this school now gives the faculty more opportunity for the making of policy than do the written documents, or the customs, of any of the other institutions studied. Under new provisions the faculty now includes the administrative officers of the college, professors, associate professors, assistant professors, instructors, substitute instructors, full-time special instructors, four critic teachers elected by the staff of permanent critic teachers, and any other full-time professional personnel which the faculty shall elect by majority vote. New rules allow for someone other than the dean to preside at faculty meetings and give only suspensive veto power to the dean. This veto is to hold over until the next monthly meeting of the faculty at which a two-thirds vote may override it. The steering committee for which the constitution provides has essentially the same power as that given to executive committees at "A," except that its members are elected, not appointed from a panel chosen by the faculty as at "A," and that they may at any time be removed by a majority vote of the faculty.

One of the other provisions of this constitution which is not to be found in law or custom at any one of the other schools relates to the selection of department heads and of the dean. In the case of a vacancy in the deanship of a department, the member of the department "shall choose a committee with a view to sharing the responsibility for the appointment of a new chairman." In the case of a vacancy in the office of the dean, the faculty "shall elect a committee to confer with the president and the board with a view to sharing the responsibility for the selection of the dean."

It is, however, in the matter of promotion that this constitution becomes much more specific than the customs followed or the provisions of the by-laws in the other institutions. Except for Colleges "A" and "B," promotions in each institution are left to deans and president. At "A" every college makes use of a committee, usually of full professors, to obtain recommendations for promotions. A large college at "B" has created a promotion committee to be elected by the faculty to which professors, associate professors, and assistant professors are eligible for nomination and election. This committee meets with the dean to consider all advancements and submits to the dean a list of proposed promotions in order of preference.

Even more generous grants of power to faculties than these are provided in the constitution of a private college established recently. The most startling of these powers have chiefly to do with faculty votes of confidence in the president, deans, and chairmen of departments. At the end of each third year in office the president is required to request a vote of confidence from the faculty. The deans, whose appointments by the president must be confirmed by a two-thirds vote of the faculty, are also directed to request a vote of confidence from the college senate. Just as surprising to the faculty members of many institutions is the provision that the faculty shall have as associate, or nonvoting members, two representatives from the student body. It is true, of course, that several outstanding colleges of education have also instituted this practice as well as the further one of adding student members to each of its standing committees.

In six of the eight institutions discussed above, then, fairly recent minor or major revisions of procedure indicate that faculty members have made gains in the nature and extent of opportunities to participate in the direction of institutional affairs. In each case, notwithstanding the alleged or actual reluctance of faculties to concern themselves about the details of management, professors have voted to assume wider responsibilities in administration. In spite of the objection of those who maintain that the faculty which so votes will only encumber itself with duties which the administrator who gets paid for the job should perform, most of the faculties under review have insisted upon the inclusion of such provisions as "suspensive vetos," "two-thirds majorities," "nomination and election by secret ballot," the election of department chairmen, and for presiding officers other than deans. These faculties appear to believe that the irritation and delay caused by the use of detailed and prescribed machinery are not too great a price to pay for recognized guarantees of the rights of self-government.

In five of the eight institutions discussed there is evidence to show that organizations not mentioned in college constitutions and by-laws have exerted influence in the direction of more democratic practices in school administration. There are those who deplore the use of such associations in this way, since they exist outside the "community of scholars" and frequently do not accord representation to administrative officers. The material in this chapter, which indicates that the rights accorded faculties are uneven and uncertain, and that in Chapter XIV to the effect that in practically all colleges there is no real delegation of control of personnel and budget matters, at least raises the question as to how some faculties can acquire the right to greater participation without employing extraconstitutional organizations to do so.

Conclusion

It is asserted by many faculty members that the councils, senates, congresses, or policy bodies, for which most constitutions provide, are sometimes so controlled by administrators that any proposal in a meeting of one of them for a shift in the prerogatives of administration may prove harmful to the future of the one who offers it. It is this situation which has been at least partly responsible for the organization of many members of college faculties into associations peculiarly their own. This is not to say that, even in meetings of these associations, the advocacy of measures which are regarded as inimical to the administration may not cause harmful criticism of individuals. Perhaps the final solution of this problem rests with professors and administrators like those in some of the institutions discussed above who have evolved ways in which a teacher's peers make the crucial decisions about his career.

The most widely known of the extraconstitutional organizations is the American Association of University Professors which reported on January 1, 1949, a membership of 33,638 in 792 institutions,[1] or 24.1 per cent of the total number of faculty members in institutions of higher education in 1944.[2] While much of the work of the national organization is related to the problem of academic freedom, local chapters have made frequent studies and recommendations about faculty welfare and general institutional policies, often in situations in which faculty members in recognized institutional bodies would have found it difficult to act.

College locals of the American Federation of Teachers have also sometimes been able to bring about action which could not have been achieved by instructors acting through recognized channels. In one instance, a local was able to focus attention on inequalities in the treatment of assistants so that remedial measures were quickly taken. A recent study of faculty locals indicates, however, that faculty labor unionism

[1] *American Association of University Professors Bulletin* (Vol. 35, p. 176, Spring, 1949).
[2] The President's Commission on Higher Education. *Higher Education for American Democracy: Resource Data* (Vol. 6, p. 36, 1948).

exists in only 29 institutions and that it is growing very slowly. It is concluded in the study that this slow growth is due in part to the fact that higher institutions are increasingly providing forms of "democratic or semidemocratic" procedure to deal with matters of rank, salary, tenure, and promotion.[3]

To the extent that the results of a study of the organization of faculties in colleges in a midwestern area can be used as an indication of a trend, it may be tentatively concluded that in general wider faculty participation in administration is being achieved. During the past ten years a great deal of effort has been expended in the preparation of constitutions and in the establishment of precedents which grant to faculties, rather than to administrators, the right to initiate policies and recommendations concerned with the curriculum and student affairs, and with staff selection, promotion, evaluation, and reward. The makers of these customs and constitutions seem to have little fear that the many safeguards to faculty prerogatives will prove burdensome. The administrators who work with them appear to feel that the position of leader in a society of self-governing professionals is more to be desired than that held by the administrator who makes decisions without benefit of counsel from his colleagues.

[3] "Labor Unionism in American Colleges," by I. A. Derbigny, in *School and Society* (60:174, March 5, 1949).

CHAPTER IX

COMPOSITION OF GOVERNING BOARDS

C L A U D E   E G G E R T S E N

University of Michigan

THERE are two recurring issues which have occupied those who would further democratize the administration of American higher education through changes in the governing boards of colleges and universities. These are: How can boards be made more representative of the community? How can faculties be accorded guaranteed responsibilities in the formation and operation of institutional policy?

The contention of Thorstein Veblen[1] that ". . . the discretionary control in matters of university policy now rests finally in the hands of business-men" has been supported by the findings of several students. In a recent study Beck[2] concludes that one of the shortcomings of the governing boards of thirty universities was their class structure.

The findings of this study have shown unmistakably that the majority of the membership of these governing boards (at least 71 per cent) was restricted to a single major social class—the class that might

[1] *The Higher Learning in America,* by Thorstein Veblen (New York: B. W. Heubsch, 1918, p. 64).

[2] *Men Who Control Our Universities,* by Hubert Park Beck (New York: King's Crown Press, 1947, p. 143).

be roughly identified as the "proprietary" class. . . . The remaining 29 per cent, who might be thought of as constituting a minority group of these boards, belonged predominantly to the traditionally conservative professions, namely: lawyers and judges, engineers, physicians and surgeons, and clergymen. No typical small tradesman or clerk was found on any board studied and only one representative of the so-called "working class" or "proletariat," a labor union official.

In another recent work,[3] "unique in that it is the first of its kind attempted from the point of view of governing boards," McAllister is unwilling to agree with the assumption, which he believes is implicit in studies of the composition of boards of trustees like that made by Beck, that a predominance of business and professional men on boards is undesirable.

It is intimated that professional and business representatives are so devoted to a narrow, partisan class point of view as to be incapable of unselfishly forwarding the best interests of the institution.

He believes that changes in the composition of boards in a ten-year period and in board policies and procedures "completely alters the picture."

This attitude of McAllister, who was President of the Association of Governing Boards of State Universities and Allied Institutions at the time he wrote, is also revealed in his disapproval of Beck's proposal for "the democratization of university control." Beck suggested that the university board should be made up of 13 members: 8 representatives of the public, 2 each of business, the professions, agriculture, and wage earners, and 5 from the university, including representatives of the faculty, the alumni, and student body.[4] McAllister objects on the ground that there is little reason to believe that members chosen by labor would prove more able or less selfish than those selected by any other group. He also

[3] *Inside the Campus*, by Charles E. McAllister (New York: Fleming H. Revell Company, 1948, pp. 11–12).

[4] Beck, *op. cit.*, p. 151.

expresses the opinion that campus politics might too greatly influence faculty members appointed to such a board and that student representation on it would prove of doubtful value.[5]

THE ISSUE ON THE COMPOSITION OF BOARDS

The principles of democratic administration advocated in this *Yearbook* seem to be more in harmony with Beck's proposal than with the doubts expressed by McAllister. The issue is not whether the representatives of one group might prove more unselfish or able than the representatives of another. It is whether capable persons from every occupational or social category should be considered available for places on governing boards as they now seem not to be. That they should be so considered is supported by the view that every person and group vitally concerned in decisions should have some opportunity to help make them. Who is not now vitally concerned with the operation of higher institutions, especially public ones, which have so close a relationship to national welfare? The increasing number of young people from all occupational and social groupings who have attended colleges and universities since V-J Day have made all classes of Americns assume a new and intimate interest in many problems of higher education. To deny them the representation which would grant a legitimate voice in the solution of these problems would seem to be an unwise public policy.

In a society dedicated to the view that the decisions which best serve our purposes and most effectively tap our resources are those in which the largest possible number of citizens participate, it is only reasonable that we should support governing boards so composed that they represent all groups in the population. There are those, of course, who think that the brains of 100,000,000 persons are not better than a se-

[5] McAllister, *op. cit.*, p. 12.

lected 1,000,000 when they regard 99,000,000 persons as muttonheads. But we have committed ourselves to the contrary for too long to make it possible, even if we thought it desirable, to alter the basic assumption that the more who work on a problem the more satisfactory its solution is likely to be. It is maintained here, therefore, that although it may not be desirable to divide our population into classes Beck mentions, for the purpose of selecting appointees to boards it is highly desirable to build a public opinion favorable to the selection of representatives of all groups and against the view that successful businessmen are almost the only promising candidates for positions as university trustees.

It is not a matter of believing that representatives of one class would prove more or less able or selfish than those of another. It is not thought that trustees who have business affiliations would consciously strive to deprive young people from labor and other groups of the opportunities ordinarily extended to young adults from homes maintained through business and professional activity. It is suggested, however, that the vocational experiences of businessmen may not give them the background necessary to understand the problems faced by scholars, or by certain groups of students. It may be, for example, that the person with the most to contribute to the solution of a problem, like that of furnishing free lunch in the public schools, may be the one whose friend's children need the nourishment, not necessarily the one who must pay the taxes, or the one who has been to college. Should we rely exclusively on the fraternity alumnus to understand the needs of students in a campus cooperative house? Is it wise to rest satisfied with the decisions of a board made up of persons oriented to the demands of business in respect to the treatment of the ever-recurring group of students of vociferously unorthodox economic views?

It may not be too much to say that the selection of trustees almost exclusively from a single major social class is an anachronism of contemporary political life. It may be a relic of that former period when the rich, and the well-born, and the able were considered the only fit managers of public affairs. It may belong to the same category of outworn usages as does the property qualifications for voters in local school board elections. Is there any reason to believe that the farmer, railroad worker, miner, druggist, or haberdasher, who is regarded as a likely public servant in city, state, or national government, as legislator or executive, would not prove adequate to the challenge of a position on a governing board? The principal reason advanced against the membership of such men is that only a man who has been formally educated should be asked to serve on boards of education. The fallacy in this is that the board member is or ought to be a policy-maker in terms of public needs, a role to be filled by a good citizen of any occupation. When the institution needs an official to put a policy into effect it should get professionally trained persons for the task.

Ought the chief considerations in the choice of board members to be those related to occupation, wealth, income, age, sex, religion, politics, education, place of residence, or family connections, as they now so often appear to be? Perhaps they might much better be those observed by voters when public servants are chosen for other offices. Able and sincere representatives of the whole people are what are required, not persons clearly attached to some special interest. A plan, like that of Beck mentioned above, which would make each board member distinctly a representative of labor, or business, or of the professions, might increase factionalism and confusion on boards and in college staffs. On the other hand, a widespread acceptance of the idea that persons from any group are to be considered available for appointment or election to boards would avoid this danger and help to make boards more representative of the whole citizenry.

FACULTY REPRESENTATION ON BOARDS

To hold that, while boards might preferably be composed of representatives of all the people they ought to allow for some special representation of the faculty, is not as contradictory as it first appears. Society expects the teacher and researchers who compose faculties to possess the imagination, initiative, and intellectual equipment to enable them to work from the known to the unknown. It has long been willing to accord them many of the freedoms indispensable to this type of activity in recognition of the fact that original work will flourish best in an atmosphere of permissiveness. For much the same reasons certain professional groups have been extended virtually full power to regulate their practices. To recognize that those who instruct and conduct experimental studies in higher institutions should have a real part in making the decisions which concern them is merely an affirmation and extension of the privileges generally accorded professional workers.

It is not unwise for society to handicap the efforts of those it maintains in higher institutions at such heavy cost by withholding such privileges? Is it economical to reject the aid of available persons trained in the solution of problems? It would seem foolish to give so generously, and then in sudden niggardly and distrustful spirit to hold back that *sine qua non* of creative work, the right of self-direction. How is it possible to justify grants to faculty members of great actual and potential power for good or bad, in social and natural sciences, in research and teaching, if the persons to whom such grants are made are not to be trusted to vote on changes in rank and salary? What profit can there be in risking dissatisfaction in the ranks of those whose contributions may have unusual significance, through a failure to consult them about policies which affect them? Is it reasonable to allow the so-called practical man of business to use authority in such fashion that the public investment in experts does not pay as well as it might if their services were fully utilized?

This is indeed a difficult suggestion for those to accept who think of college teachers as employees and of trustees as employers. It is clear to them that power flows from the people to the trustees and that a relinquishment of authority to employees would be a betrayal of a trust. Yet, considerations such as those presented in the above paragraphs indicate that the task of administering institutions most effectively and efficiently for the welfare of all can be carried out only by a partial rejection of the principle of a hierarchy of commands. This realization is all the more difficult to achieve when it is also understood that no conditional allocation of the prerogative of self-discipline, no matter how deeply imbedded in constitutions it may seem to be, will achieve the purpose. Only grants of the powers of self-government made in such a way that faculties may rely upon their continuance will procure for society the highest returns from its investment in higher education.

The way to such a solution of the problem of faculty representation may be somewhat less difficult than it may first appear. There is a beginning in the fact that, while almost no faculty members have any formal assignments to boards of their own institutions, faculty sentiment is assiduously sought and scrupulously reported to the boards of many schools. In Chapter VII of this *Yearbook*, practices of this type in a number of institutions are cited and in Chapter XIV a few examples are given of college administrations which proceed upon what are called the bases of consultation and participation, even to the point of having faculty members serve on boards.

It is true, then, that the idea of the participation of the faculty in what have been regarded as exclusively board affairs is beginning to gain some recognition. That it is only a beginning is clear from the replies obtained by McAllister to the question, "Does Board have close contact with faculty. . . ?" Most of the responses were "no," or "through the president." Only four said "yes." McAllister concludes[6] that it would be unwise to modify the rule, thus discovered, of almost no consultation of board and faculty.

When it comes to board contacts with faculty, students, and alumni, the original opinion of the author was that such contacts should be encouraged. However, a study of the conditions existing at the eighty-nine colleges and universities considered in this report leads me to revise that opinion. The less personal contact there is between board members and faculty members . . . the better. . . . There is a trend in some institutions today to have more faculty participation in recommendations for appointments and promotions. . . . Unfortunately, in the institutions where the faculties have considerable power in naming deans or recommending changes in rank, the procedure has not always worked well.

From these findings and recommendations, then, it is clear that the proper avenue of communication between faculty and regents is considered to be the president. However much this may have been true in the past, is it still true in a time of swollen enrollments, larger faculties, and of new and specialized functions? Can the theory be maintained in the face of the appointment of military, political, and business leaders to presidencies?

Under such circumstances, assuming that presidents genuinely wish to do what is best for faculties, how can they understand faculty needs, much less properly evaluate and

[6] McAllister, *op. cit.*, p. 214.

express them to governing boards? That there is a gulf difficult to bridge between faculty and president was asserted recently by Kenneth I. Brown,[7] President of the Association of American Colleges and of Denison University, when he said that the faculty and administration in American colleges are divided into two distinct classes, with an ever-present danger of the occurrence of the kind of flareups that exists in industry.

On the one hand, then, presidents are not to be considered as the proper agencies through which the faculty may participate in administration, and faculty representation on boards is not legal or desirable. On the other hand, good public policy demands that the resources of faculty members be used in university affairs and teachers be not inhibited in their work by annoyances which could be removed through consultation. What seems to be a reasonable compromise of these two sets of contradictory facts?

Perhaps a key to a compromise is to be found in a recent statement by an administrative official, fully cognizant of the problem. He says that neither the president nor the vice-president at his institution could hope to win favorable action of the trustees on a recommendation about curriculum, staff, or student body unless it were accompanied by a statement from the dean and staff of the college of colleges concerned. The board of the institution in question has long held that the prerogatives which belong to the faculties must be safeguarded.

The objections to this solution on the part of those who hope to extend the participation of the faculty in administration are two. First, the right may be legally abrogated by any board at any time. Second, the making of decisions affecting the entire university—with the decision resting upon advice offered by a single college—has the effect of forcing entire col-

[7] *New York Times,* January 11, 1949.

lege faculties to follow practices with which they disagree. The way out of the first difficulty is for faculties to insist that rights be clearly spelled out in by-laws and constitutions, and to maintain associations to keep vigilant watch over the prerogatives thus gained. The solution to the second problem may be for the faculties of all teaching units to describe the kinds of decisions upon which they desire a voice and press for a statement about them to be included in the by-laws and constitutions.

The People to be Represented on the Board

Finally, the type of control over higher institutions which will in the long run reflect the aspirations of those who support them is that which is representative of all the people. Changes should be made in existing legal structures and attitudes which are in part responsible for the numerical dominance of businessmen on governing boards. For the present this may best be done by reeducating the people of each state about requirements for appointment or election. Faculties might well make this reeducation one of their extracurricular tasks.

If society is to obtain a full return on its investment in higher education, new and better ways must be found to utilize the varied abilities of faculty members in institutional planning. Further, faculties should be trusted to the point that they have virtually a free hand in creating the atmosphere in which they are expected to make contributions to teaching and scholarship.

PART THREE
The Responsibility of Administration

CHAPTER X

SELECTING AND APPRAISING PERSONNEL

GLADYS A. WIGGIN

University of Maryland

A GREAT university faculty is a distinctive Joseph's coat of many colors and materials. It may be fashioned by artistry and technique into a garment which can be told from all others by only a casual inspection of its particular arrangement of hues and pieces. Such unique coats have been worn by universities of distinction in five continents, through eight centuries of history.

This institutional pattern, perhaps because of its multiform character, has never been subjected to the analysis which its uniqueness deserves. The art of the faculty-builder-craftsman has been learned anew by each succeeding head of an institution of higher learning. Certain skills and techniques of an earlier age or another contemporary leader have been selected for use by the new administrator. Certain principles of operation in the building reappear in other patterns in succeeding societies. But few aspiring doctoral candidates or idol-breaking researchers have inquired into the mysteries employed by the artist-craftsmen of higher education in their tasks. Instead, mediocre and distinguished laymen, presidents, deans, professors have stated their faiths in particular elements of their crafts. These faiths may be in persons: "progress comes mainly from the faculties"; or in techniques: a faculty "is a ruminating animal; chewing a cud a long time, slowly bringing it into a digestible condition"; or in instruments: "In each of these departments democratic procedures in the selection and promotion of personnel have been practiced."

To a member of a modern faculty, dedicated to the use of tested hypotheses, these faith-ridden statements are both maddening and illuminating. They throw light, but what light shall be judged brightest? They propose truths, but which truths shall be judged sound? They suggest hypotheses, but which hypotheses have been validated? In order to isolate the statements which indicate elements in selecting and appraising personnel, there must be developed criteria by which to judge the greatness of institutions, administrators, and professors.

Proposed Criteria of Institutional Distinction

The first criterion is that of tradition by which certain men have been judged great through their parts in founding the modern American university.[1] The statements and careers of such men as Charles W. Eliot and William Rainey Harper have therefore been studied to determine the characteristics of great university presidents and teachers.

The second criterion has been derived by asking chairmen of history departments of colleges and universities approved by the Association of American Universities to name the distinguished professors of American history since 1875. Personalities of professors appearing on at least one fourth of the lists have been probed for qualities which seemed to have made them great professors.

---

[1] See such historical studies as *The College Charts Its Course*, by R. Freeman Butts (New York and London: McGraw-Hill Book Company, Inc., 1939).

The third criterion has been developed by asking five men of varying backgrounds and wide experience in education to rank the outstanding graduate schools of education of the last twenty years, and to indicate whether in the last ten years these schools have been going up, going down, or remaining on a level. Analysis of staff training of members of certain institutions appearing on lists of all five judges has been used in this statement.

The fourth criterion is a series of conclusions reached by Visher[2] in his study of institutions in which starred scientists received their doctoral degrees. Before exploring the leads from these four criteria it might be well to state that, for lack of time, none of the studies based on these criteria has been exhausted.

PERSONNEL AND THE UNIVERSITY PATTERN

When American university faculties which have been judged great are looked at in their totalities the patterns they present are strikingly apparent. Though each institutional pattern differs from all others in color and design, the process by which the pieces of the pattern are fitted together into an intricate mosaic is surprisingly constant from one institution to another. A weak president selecting the pieces will produce a hodgepodge; a weak professor fitting into the design will jar the sensibilities of the observer. The principle underlying the development of the great institutional pattern appears therefore to be the starting point for a discussion of selection and appraisal of college and university faculties.

The first element in that pattern is clear. A university is an institution in which human ingenuity and intellect are allowed free rein. Universities become great to the extent that in them is created a situation whereby the uniqueness of

[2] *Scientists Starred*, 1903–1943, in "American Men of Science," by Stephen Sargent Visher (Baltimore: The Johns Hopkins Press, 1947).

the personalities of the faculty and their creativity and learning ability can be utilized most effectively. A great university creates the situation in which individuals may withdraw into their own personalities and come forth again into a community of minds against which their unique minds may rub and give off sparks. In accord with a description of a great university in terms of its humanness, the principle for its development is that the institutional pattern shall be an integrated whole conditioned by the individual excellence of each piece in the pattern: a great president, a great dean, great professors, great students.

The thesis of the integrated effect can be amply supported. The great presidents had not one good man, but as was said of William Rainey Harper, "a galaxy of stars." Techniques employed by the great presidents were addressed on the one hand to knowing the idiosyncrasies of their staffs and on the other hand to selecting more staff in terms of a great design. With unfailing regularity Charles W. Eliot attended and presided over the meetings of all faculties in Harvard University. This innovation in the actions of a president he considered the most important single change made in the administration of Harvard.[3] Andrew D. White[4] of Cornell makes mention of a particular rejuvenation only when fortunately he had found "three men who enabled us to tide our agricultural department over those dark days, in which we seemed to be playing 'Hamlet' with Hamlet left out." Perhaps subconsciously believing this integrative effect to have practical applications, Harper of Chicago took fifteen men in the sciences from Clark University at one time.[5]

---

[3] *Charles W. Eliot*, by Henry James, Vol. I, p. 243 (Boston and New York: Houghton Mifflin Co., 1930).

[4] *Autobiography of Andrew Dickson White* with portraits, Vol. I, p. 369 (New York: The Century Co., 1922).

[5] *William Rainey Harper: First President of the University of Chicago*, by Thomas Wakefield Goodspeed (Chicago: The University of Chicago Press, 1928).

An effect of the integrating factor can be ascertained by studying the institutions which have conferred doctorates on the starred scientists.

About 1630 of the starred scientists, or nearly two-thirds, obtained doctorates (not honorary) from American universities. More than half of these degrees were conferred by the four leaders, Harvard 274, Johns Hopkins 238, Chicago 194, and Columbia 175.[6]

Furthermore, these doctorates are not spread evenly among the decades but bunch in decades and cluster around particular sciences in which faculties have been strong.

The pattern of institutions at which ranking American history professors have taught indicates the persistence of the integrating effect in this limited area of the social sciences. Note in Table I that Harvard appears four times in a list of ten institutions with which these men are identified, and compare that with Harvard's reputation as the ranking institution for the study of history.

TABLE I.—RANKING AMERICAN HISTORY PROFESSORS
SINCE 1875

Name of professor	No. of lists on which name appears	University with which the professor is identified as teacher
Turner, Frederick Jackson	130	Wisconsin and Harvard
Dunning, William A.	65	Columbia
Channing, Edward	60	Harvard
Adams, Herbert Baxter	51	Johns Hopkins
Andrew, Charles M.	51	Yale
Bolton, Herbert E.	46	California
Schlesinger, Arthur M.	40	Harvard
Dodd, William E.	39	Chicago
Hart, Albert B.	38	Harvard

As a corollary of the principle of the integrating effect, the president of the great university must be first and fore-

[6] Visher, *op. cit.,* p. 25.

most an educational leader. The present craze for boosting businessmen, lawyers, and generals into high places in colleges and universities is likely to result in sharp deterioration of institutional patterns. It is not that an institution is the long shadow of a man, but that an experienced university administrator must be at hand to create those academic circumstances in which great professors and great students can work. Samuel Eliot Morison[7] points out this educational potency of the administrative head when he discusses crucial factors in building the great department of history at Harvard university.

A university president whose only experience with an army had been service as a youth in a reserve unit would never be asked to lead an army into battle; the disastrous effects on the lives of men and nations would be so obvious as to preclude any such consideration. Putting in charge of a university a commander of troops whose only connection with a university had been as an undergraduate student is equally disastrous to the development of our social institutions. It is a trend which should be fought against vigorously by those who are working for the expanding social usefulness of the university.

The master craftsmen of the great universities have been educational statesmen having clear-cut notions of the functions of a university, wide acquaintance with the several fields on which a university must draw for staff, and a zest for championing unpopular movements designed to improve society and their own universities. Their major concerns have been in the field of university administration.

Most of these educational leaders have exhibited their flair for organizing university work long before they have been called to presidencies. It was said of Charles W. Eliot when he was still an assistant professor of chemistry that "in

[7] Letter of Samuel Eliot Morison to the author, July 4, 1949.

everything connected with university administration, from devising written examinations to overseeing the construction of a new building, the President was apt to ask Mr. Eliot to do it, and it was done." [8] Mr. Eliot helped the president make up the docket of business for corporation meetings, secured for the Department of Literature a large order of books and periodicals from Germany, prepared a plan for the Lawrence Scientific School. On his trip to Europe in 1863–65 he displayed an insatiable curiosity about organization and methods employed in educational institutions, including how floors were laid and how the lycées kept their systems of accounts.[9]

The Cornell idea was already simmering in young Andrew White's breast when he was still a Hobart undergraduate bitterly reviewing the inadequacies of the teaching force and equipment of the little college. When he was a young man in Syracuse his ideal university was already a written plan to which his friend George William Curtis referred at White's inauguration.[10] David Starr Jordan had been president of Indiana University and leader of many scientific expeditions before becoming first president of Stanford University.[11] By the age of 30, William Rainey Harper was conducting six schools of Hebrew and teaching one thousand students through an elaborate system of correspondence education. The abilities of these men were exhibited early, and they succeeded to presidencies in the age span 35–45. Although Visher does not refer specifically to administrative ability of the great presidents, he does point out the high coincidence of distinguished presidents at the times

[8] *Three Centuries of Harvard* 1636–1936, by Samuel Eliot Morison (Cambridge: Harvard University Press, 1942, p. 325).

[9] James, *op. cit.*, pp. 70, 71, 95, 120, 122.

[10] White, *op. cit.*, p. 292.

[11] *The Days of a Man*, by David Staff Jordan (New York: World Book Company, Vol. I, 1922).

when the greatest numbers of starred scientists have received their degrees. He does mention the factor of youth which he says puts a president close to his faculty and students in ideas and interests.[12]

How the Great Presidents Secured Great Professors

To the task of designing the institutional pattern these great presidents brought a wide acquaintance with academic worlds in American and foreign universities. If their universities were to exhibit the widest possible display of unique talents then logically these talents should be recruited from as many different faculties as possible. Harper reached out to Freiburg for a historian, to Minnesota for a dean, to Cornell for a professor of Latin, to Colby for a sociologist. Before the end of his probationary period as president of Harvard, Eliot had appointed among the Harvard men, one in philosophy from Göttingen and California, another in botany from Yale, still another in entomology from Königsberg, and a teacher of French from the Massachusetts Institute of Technology. While still president of Indiana University, David Starr Jordan saw the importance of securing faculty members who had lived in and understood the Middle West; but he required them to take advanced training in eastern or European universities.[13] Henry Tappan believed that "as the republic of letters overlaps national boundaries," foreign professors might be happily employed to assist in multiplying native scholars.[14]

This mark of a great president and corollary of the integrative effect might be stated as a principle of selection of personnel. Inbreeding of faculty may bear an inverse relationship to the greatness of an institutional pattern. Al-

[12] Visher, *op. cit.*, pp. 36–37.

[13] Jordan, *op. cit.*, p. 295.

[14] *Henry Philip Tappan* Philosopher and University President, by Charles M. Perry (Ann Arbor: University of Michigan Press, 1933, p. 234).

though this is only one minor piece of evidence in support of the principle, results of inbreeding can be seen in Table II which summarizes staff training of members of four great schools of education. The institutions tending to remain on a level or go up in standing in the last ten years of the twenty years under study have a lower percentage of their staff members with doctoral degrees from the teaching institution.

TABLE II.—DOCTORAL TRAINING OF FACULTY MEMBERS OF GREAT GRADUATE SCHOOLS OF EDUCATION

Institution	*Percentage of faculty with doctoral degrees secured in institutions in which they are teachers in the years*			
	1928–29	1933–34	1938–39	1943–44
Tending to be going down				
Institution A	71	79	75	76
Institution B	45	56	33	39
Tending to remain on a level or go up				
Institution C	26	26	32	28
Institution D	25	32	29	35

The appreciation of the great university presidents for the qualities which make for great teachers stemmed from their own apprenticeships as professors. They had all been successful teachers who knew the academic worlds in enough specificity to be able to judge both teaching and research abilities. They had published researches, and statements on questions of public importance. David Starr Jordan[15] maintained that a man's teaching should continue even after the man became a university president.

Again, as I have already implied, to judge the work of scholars accurately he himself (the president) should be a scholar, which condition he can maintain only through some form of actual research.

[15] Jordan, *op. cit.*, p. 298.

Without personal effort toward the extension of knowledge, he is likely to fall out of harmony with scholarship and thus fail in his most important duty—the selection of progressive men.

Each of the great presidents was broad enough in his thinking to preserve a decent respect for disciplines other than his own. Most of them looked on subject fields as instruments for developing students and professors, and as instruments there could be no evaluation of them except in terms of the expertness with which they were used and their usefulness to the purposes of the university. The sentiments of the great presidents in this regard can be summed up in a statement of President White's:[16]

As to non-resident professors, I secured in London Goldwin Smith, who had recently distinguished himself by his works as a historian and as regius professor of history at Oxford; and I was successful in calling Dr. James Law, who, though a young man, had already made himself a name in veterinary science. It seemed to many a comical juxtaposition, and various witticisms were made at my expense over the statement that I had "brought back an Oxford professor and a Scotch horse-doctor." But never were selections more fortunate.

So far there have been described certain traits of great presidents which are but peripheral to the firm core of their greatness. The essence of their greatness is in the sweep of their educational philosophies and the strength of their educational courage. To them all, a university was an institution whose unique function in a democracy was that of standard bearer on the front line of intellectual endeavor and social reform. Henry Tappan's philosophical university was somewhat antecedent to the universities of the other great presidents; but in Tappan's notion of it were the seeds of greatness.

It is easy to get up scholasticism under prescription, but investigation and productive thought must be free as birds upon the wing—

[16] White, *op. cit.*, p. 339.

they must bear themselves along by their own native vigor, in their own native element. And we must run the risk of flying in the wrong direction sometimes, or we can have no flying at all, unless it be the wretched flying of a decoy-pigeon—fluttering within the limits of a string held by the hand of its master.[17]

Freeing professors for research as well as for public duties and providing them with graduate as well as undergraduate students that their challenges might be greater, was part and parcel of the process of making the university an instrument in freeing the whole people from the results of their own ignorance. A democracy to be at its best must make use of the abilities of all; so the university must extend its curricula to meet the needs of more varied students; scholarships must be provided to reduce the unhappy results of economic discrimination; professors must be recruited from as varied academic areas as possible; techniques such as the university press and the extension division must be devised to allow scope for professors' talents and service to the people. The university, whether publicly or privately supported, must be understood as the crown of a system of elementary and secondary schools from which the universities must constantly draw new sources of strength. Most of the great presidents did their part in developing public schools and publicly supported teacher training. Above all, when there had been stated a principle of university organization which was central to the purpose of the institution as an instrument of democratic social reform, there could be no retreating from the principle though the critics of the university's purposes be baying on the trail of the offending president. It is because of this last stipulation that Daniel Coit Gilman must be dropped from the list of the great presidents while Charles W. Eliot assumes a more exalted place. Gilman fled from the California politicians who threatened to engulf his academic career to

[17] Quoted in Perry, *op. cit.*, p. 218.

the safe haven of a new university where the president with wealth and power behind him could do no wrong. Eliot stepped into a bed of tradition at Harvard and blandly trampled that tradition underfoot though he knew full well that for the first sixteen years of his stay at Harvard his stomping put his tenure in constant jeopardy. The circumstances made Gilman; but Eliot made the circumstances. The philosophies and character of most of these men are epitomized in this statement by President Charles R. Van Hise of Wisconsin, a descendant of the great presidents:

In the university men are trained to regard economic and social questions as problems to be investigated by the inductive methods, and in their solutions to *aim at what is best for the whole people rather than at what is favorable to the interests with which they chance to be connected.* . . . Soon such men will be found in every city and hamlet, leading the fight against corruption and misrule, and, even more important and vastly more difficult, *leading in constructive advance.* In these men lies, in great measure, the hope of a peaceful solution of the great questions deeply concerning the nation, some of which are scarcely less momentous than was that of slavery.[18]

FACTORS IN INSTITUTIONAL DISTINCTION

So far in this discussion it appears that there are two sets of standards for judging an institutional pattern: one has to do with the many-faceted design as it achieves its own peculiar harmony, and the other is concerned with the individual excellence and uniqueness of each piece in the pattern.

In addition to factors so far discussed, another factor which will influence the design will be the character of the institutional pattern. Thus there are probably a set of function qualifications which all members of selected staffs will have. A great school of education has set up for itself the objective of working with the public schools; therefore each staff mem-

[18] Quoted in Butts, *op. cit.*, pp. 228–229. (Italics in the original).

ber must of necessity have had some type of successful public school experience. A great department of history feels that its students must have experience in medieval history; therefore the new professor to be appointed must be an expert in medieval history. A great college of agriculture believes that the time has come to extend its usefulness from the productive to the economic field. Therefore the basic consideration in selecting a new staff member is that the contemplated member's field of concentration be in cooperatives. The problem of the design is relatively simple when decision on its character is kept within departments operating under a single budget. When interests cut across department or college lines the problem becomes infinitely complex. The department of history urgently needs a medievalist; but the school of agriculture (so its staff believes) needs a professor of cooperatives even more.

FACTORS IN PROFESSORIAL DISTINCTION

The problem of precedence of needs can only be solved in terms of another principle of designing a great university. An institutional pattern is great to the extent that faculty members from the president to the graduate assistant appreciate and accept the institution's objectives, and dedicate themselves to the expansion and modification of those objectives in terms of greater social usefulness of the institution. This implies the correlative of an appreciation on the part of every professor for the unique talents, abilities, and worth of every other professor. This kind of appreciation for one another's talents, coupled with a corresponding degree of respect for academic freedom, is credited with being a reason why first-class men are attracted to the history department at Harvard University.[19]

Prosecution of these objectives and statement of the indi-

[19] Morison letter, July 4, 1949.

vidual objectives are unique with institutions. In terms of the philosophies of the great presidents these objectives fall in the categories of service to the university student and service to the adults in the state, the nation, the world.

Choosing professors in terms of these broad areas is as complex a question as that of an analysis of human personality. There are as many kinds of professors as there are students to be taught and adults to be assisted.

This uniqueness of professors can be best illustrated by proposing a common characteristic, a proposal which appears to deny the validity of the uniqueness theory. This characteristic, however, will presently appear as a genus of which each professor may represent a different species.

Visher's considered statement[20] on teachers of starred scientists will serve to introduce one aspect of this characterisistic:

> The fluctuation in output of subsequently starred men correlates partly with the age of the leading teachers. . . . When the gap in age, scholarly achievement and outlook between professor and student is large, the close fellowship which apparently is almost essential for effective stimulation can seldom occur.

In the words of a great president, there are only two types of professors: young men and men who never grow old. Lest judgment be faulty as to whether a man old in age might still remain young in.ideas, most of the great presidents preferred to intersperse their faculties with very young men of promise.

This factor of youth, however, is only one aspect of the characteristic which must persuade its case again and again. Its manifestation can best be unfolded by recalling a familiar theme in faculty discussions.

"Dr. G. C. Bloodtree is a marvelous man in the laboratory [chemistry, engineering, history] but he can't teach."

"What do you mean, can't teach?"

[20] Visher, *op. cit.*, p. 38.

"Well, he can't put his stuff across in the classroom."

"Doesn't Dr. Bloodtree have any students?"

"Oh yes, he always has some doctoral candidates hanging around."

"Do these candidates ever amount to anything?"

"As a matter of fact, they do. They are usually known as fairly distinguished research men and professors. But old Bloodtree [very emphatically now] can't teach worth a damn!"

It is a source of great satisfaction to know that the evidence at hand admits of a more fundamental characteristic of good teaching than ability to perform in a classroom. This characteristic, simply stated, is the ability to stimulate students. The quality of this stimulation will be unique to the professor who is the source of the inspiration. In relation to teaching in the sciences Visher says[21] "it appears that a teacher who is deeply interested in his individual student is almost essential."

In the case of the graduate professor, the quality of thinking which the professor brings to his task may well determine the quality of his inspiration to others. Students of the great history professors report those professors as raising more questions than they answer; as persuading for an evolutionary rather than an absolute definition of truth; as opening up new areas for research rather than beating out old paths. According to those who studied at Hopkins under Herbert Baxter Adams:

Men who came out of that period have repeatedly spoken of the exhilaration felt in the new opportunities of research, the close contact with the expansion of human knowledge; and the consciousness of the unique experiment in which they were engaged.[22]

[21] *Ibid.*, pp. 35–36.
[22] *American Masters of Social Science*, Howard W. Odum, editor (New York: Henry Holt and Company, 1927, p. 106).

Avery O. Craven[23] has pointed out that the key to the success of Professor William E. Dodd as a teacher was his ability to stimulate and to suggest. ". . . Professor Dodd could point out fields for profitable investigation and open paths of approach to them with a skill such as few American historians have ever shown."

Conclusions regarding great teaching have been reached by the writers of memoirs of five of the great teachers of American history. To the hostesses of Cambridge, Edward Channing turned polite refusals until they stopped asking him to dinner. To his colleagues he remained something of an enigma. He sacrificed the ordinary pleasures of social intercourse, participation in good causes, and monetary temptations to the writing of his great history of the United States. To his students, however, his devotion was sustained and genuine. They were free to trouble him at all hours and for long periods of time with personal or academic difficulties—"his own students were his friends for life." [24]

Willaim A. Dunning and Herbert Baxter Adams were very different men from Channing except in one respect: the tribute of their students to their kindness and inspiration is if anything more lyrical. William E. Dodd had the power to make students feel that they were scholars in their own right. "Even in large classes (Professor Dodd's) a surprising number came to believe that they had been singled out for especial attention and had been credited with marked ability." [25] In Frederick Jackson Turner, master teacher of them all, is unfolded that supreme gift, as Carl Becker said: [26] the ability to appreciate and spy out genius in the most obscure and

---

[23] "William E. Dodd As Teacher," by Avery O. Craven (*The University of Chicago Magazine*, 32: 8, May, 1940).

[24] *Edward Channing* A Memoir, by Samuel Eliot Morison (Reprinted from the Proceedings of the Massachusetts Historical Society, 64: May, 1931).

[25] Craven, *op. cit.*, p. 7.

[26] Odum, *op. cit.*, p. 288.

unprepossessing student. "How the rash man gambled on us to be sure, professing to see in us qualities and virtues marking us out for future *savants*." The mote in the eye of the great teacher as he looks on those most gifted of all gifted humans, his own students, is engagingly revealed in the words of Dunning to his former students who were honoring him on his succession to the presidency of the American Historical Association:[27]

You are all teachers now, and you will hand on the torch to a generation that I shall not know. It is unlikely that any of you, however much more deserving of it, will be favored with so exceptional a body of students as it has been my fortune to teach. That occurs, in the nature of things, but once in many generations. Yet I can find nothing more devoutly to pray for than that this unlikely thing may happen. . . .

For the many variants of this common characteristic of great teachers no successful measuring instrument has yet been devised. Although valuable work has been done with rating scales, these scales have largely been too narrowly conceived. They are ordinarily instruments which measure management of undergraduate classroom situations.

MEASURES OF INSTITUTIONAL DISTINCTIONS

If the thesis of the unique professor is correct, then there would be no justification for measuring a man by his competence in only one of the kinds of teaching situations in a university. Neither should there be comparisons of one professor with another in terms of a single measuring scale. There can be no countenance of fruitless arguments regarding whether the professor of the many research articles is better or worse than the effective counselor of undergraduate students; or whether the rigid conservative is more or less desirable

[27] Quoted in introduction by J. G. deRoulhac Hamilton to *Truth in History and Other Essays*, by William A. Dunning, p. xxii (New York: Columbia University Press, 1937).

than the propounder of the unorthodox. Any and all of these types of teachers are necessary if they provide stimulation for the several kinds of students with which the institution deals.

Recently a dean of a famous general college made the statement in confidence that it required a particular kind of staff to be happy in and successful at guiding and teaching a group of students at the college level who were not destined to be members of the so-called learned professions. He ventured a guess that those who were happiest in the general college faculty probably would not fit successfully into the traditional colleges. As colleges extend their notions of the boundary lines for admitting students, the numbers of rating scales for judging professorial worth will need to be correspondingly expanded. The thesis of the unique professor thus results in another principle of selection. Adherence to a standardized set of traits for selecting professors will be the undoing of a democratically based institution and force on the offending institution the anomaly of Eliot's uniform student.

Under the philosophy of the unique professor, faculty participation in selection and appraisal of professors is valuable only to the extent that the faculty are educated to the broad purposes of university teaching. When the process of education is in its incipient stage, it might be both dangerous and foolhardy for the administrator to solicit faculty advice in appointments merely from some blind adherence to a democratic myth.

When Eliot consulted individuals privately about an appointment, they were apt not to be the professors who might think themselves most intimately concerned. If, for instance, it was deplorable that old Professor Bowen should be the one and only fountain of instruction in both Philosophy and Economics, it was clear that the selection of other men to serve as correctives and antidotes and ultimately to replace him could not be guided by Bowen himself.[28]

[28] James, *op. cit.*, p. 253.

To the extent that a faculty becomes educated, it should be allowed freedom in developing a policy for selection and appraisal of faculty. Under wise leadership the increasing reliance of the administrative head on faculty advisement can become an instrument for the education of the faculty.

With the necessity for constant education and reeducation of the faculty the importance of the department head is seen in a new light. Visher[29] concludes from his study of the doctoral institutions of starred scientists that

The departmental fluctuation normally correlates with the leadership of the department. Repeatedly when an outstanding man is given leadership, the departmental output of subsequently distinguished alumni jumps.

Visher's statement would call into question the practice of rotating chairman which has been defended as a democratic technique. Although Visher's statement should not be accepted as final for all types of departments, it does suggest the danger in interpreting democracy as a set of techniques rather than as a set of goals. If a university is dedicated to the exploitation of unique abilities in terms of their social usefulness, then the practice of rotating chairmen might be utilized as a selective technique rather than as one good of itself.

Given a philosophy for a university in terms of that of the great presidents and given the conditions under which a professor may exploit his talents to the fullest, the process of appraising the individual professor is relatively simple. The professor must be appraised on the aggressiveness with which under the right type of leadership he finds his niche in the great university pattern. If he fancies himself a recluse in the laboratory but he publishes no researches and turns out few graduate students, his contributions to the design of the university may well be called into question. If he is hired as a field worker, however, and in response to the unfolding of his abilities finds

[29] Visher, *op. cit.*, page 38.

himself the center of a stimulating experience in freshman counseling, his colleagues should think long and earnestly before insisting on his carrying out the original objective of his appointment.

Selection and appraisal of personnel in institutions of higher education are the processes by which the designs for the great universities complete themselves. The details of those processes change as the institutional patterns under the hand of the educational leaders achieve new and richer forms. The objectives of that selection and appraisal remain as constant as the necessity for judging each piece in the pattern in terms of the master design.

CHAPTER XI

SECURING AND DISTRIBUTING
FINANCIAL SUPPORT

L A U R E N C E D. H A S K E W

University of Texas

H E WHO pays the piper calls the tune. Money will operate higher education, and money will, in large measure, pattern higher education. Money is power. It becomes pertinent, therefore, to examine how much power can be put back of higher education for a democracy. It becomes even more pertinent to determine the spots at which that power shall be applied, and the directions in which that power shall tend.

The challenge of democracy to higher education has three outstanding financial manifestations. In the first place, there is the manifestation of sheer size. The need for a dramatic expansion in higher education has lately been˙ documented. It will be an expansion that will embrace doubled and trebled numbers of persons within a quadrupled education opportunity: more people, more services, more costly procedures.

Second, there is the manifestation of sources. No longer can higher education be content with having enough money to run on. It is perforce concerned with the social origins and effects of its support and with the procedures employed in securing its financial well-being.

Third, there is the manifestation of budgetary distribution. The objectives set forth for higher education in the twentieth century will be realized only when college and university budgets reflect those objectives. It cannot be assumed that colleges and universities will ever have money enough to do all things that are desirable. Each year choices will have to be made under a ceiling that forces the distribution of funds according to some scheme of relative importance. A new cyclotron must be weighed against a research center in human dynamics or a continuation center building. Lip service can hardly compensate for the lack of financial support.

The current chapter, therefore, essays an exploration of these challenges to the structure of support for American higher education. Its basic thesis is that financing higher education is only one aspect of a much larger function of American society; namely, financing a democratic-tending way of life.

The Financial Support Needed

Financial support for higher education has two aspects. One aspect is the support for the colleges and universities themselves. The other is support for the persons who invest their time and energy in being students in those colleges and universities.

Support for Colleges and Universities. What will it cost to support the colleges and universities needed for higher education in the future? Estimates run from a conservative two-billion-dollar annual figure to an optimistic six-billion-dollar proposal, and strong evidence exists that this latter figure may be totally inadequate. Many complicating factors make even reasonable guesses impossible, but it may be worth while to examine some of those factors.

The enrollments in colleges and universities in the United States, even if they do no more than continue pre-World War

II trends, will perhaps not level off before they hit the 3,000,-000 figure. If a more liberal policy of student aid is followed, if geographical regions hitherto underprivileged economically continue their climb up the standard-of-living ladder, if the available labor force continues to exceed the effective demand for laborers, the leveling-off figure may well be close to 4 million. At the 1939–40 expenditure levels, adjusted to 1949 dollar-value, not much less than 3 billion dollars annually would be required to furnish college education for an enrollment of four million.

However, 1939–40 expenditure levels did not provide the ranges or the quality of services commonly demanded by those who expect higher education to become a powerful instrument of democracy. Neither did those levels provide comfort-level salaries for college teachers and research workers. Studies of individual institutions reveal the necessity for increasing current expenditures by 30 to 70 per cent if satisfactory range and quality is to be secured in the offerings of those institutions. It would seem conservative to project an expenditure level 25 per cent above that of 1939–40 in the interest of quality. This would make our total figure in the vicinity of four billions.

It may be argued, of course, that colleges and universities would save enough money for all needed increases in scope and quality by adopting truly efficient curriculum design and teaching procedures, and by avoiding wasteful duplications of offerings between colleges in the same geographical regions. Insufficient evidence exists to judge the validity of this argument *in toto*, but limited experimentation indicates that it should be accorded considerable attention.

Another factor influencing the eventual total cost of higher education is the definition of "higher." If the thirteenth and fourteenth years of schooling become an accepted and integral part of America's common school system—as most persons predict they will be—the cost of "higher" education may be reduced by forty or fifty per cent. Universal education through the fourteenth year, however, will inevitably increase the enrollments in upper division, professional, and graduate schools unless America adopts a policy of perferential selection that is foreign to its educational history up to now. In other words, while the burgeoning community college movement may bring some temporary recession in the financial support needed for traditional higher education, it does not seem likely that it will offer a means for permanent reduction of the higher education budget.

At least one other factor needs to be taken into account. Within the past three years, many new state-supported colleges have come into being, and many more have been assigned functions heretofore reserved to a very few institutions. If this is the forerunner of overextension of college facilities through catering to local pride and political pressure—as well it might be—the total cost for higher education may mount considerably over the levels already indicated. If, on the other hand, regional planning for development of higher education facilities, such as that now contemplated under the Board of Control for Southern Regional Higher Education, can gain a real foothold, the total cost can be lowered considerably.

The figures for the total cost of higher education need not be staggering, though large. They should be viewed only in context, and that context is the economic ability of the American society and the social goals of American democracy. Investment in higher education, judging by the past, pays returns in sheer dollars and cents far beyond the yields of most collective expenditures. That it will pay even greater social returns is quite possible, if it does indeed become higher education for American democracy.

Support for Students. Hungate[1] estimated that in 1937–

38, college students in the United States spent 594
dollars to live, exclusive of college fees, while atten~
lege. A similar figure for 1947–48 would doubtles~
mate 2 billion dollars. Even allowing for consi~
crease in the proportion of at-home residence by
dents in the future, a conservative estimate of cosu ~
for college students in 1965 is 3 billion 1949-value dollars.

To the actual cost of living for students some would add
"the cost of wages not earned." Thus, it is calculated that
the individual student is not only paying his cost of living but
also is investing an amount equal to that he would earn if employed gainfully. To this writer, the inclusion of such items
seems unjustified but the line of argument that favors their
inclusion does add weight to the contention that the cost of
living for a student is a genuine current expense for operating
higher education, Furthermore, it throws new light upon
who can "afford" to go to college.

In brief summary, then, it is estimated that the financial
support needed for higher education in the future aggre-
gates somewhere in the neighborhood of six to seven billion
dollars annually with only normal expenditures for capital
outlay. Where is the money coming from?

SECURING FINANCIAL SUPPORT

The democratic approach to supporting higher education
for American democracy would seem to be simple. The
money needed would be collected from all who were able
to pay, in proportion to their ability to pay, and expended to
educate all those who could profit society by participating in

[1] *Financing the Future of Higher Education*, by Thad L. Hungate (New
York: Bureau of Publications, Teachers College, Columbia University.
1946, p. 163).

[2] The foregoing estimates include only full-time students, and not those
millions of adults and youth who should be participating in higher education activities on a part-time basis.

higher education. If American society were starting afresh, such an approach might be possible. But in a society in midstream, many complicating traditions bar the obvious approach.

Higher education, in the American tradition, is only partially viewed as a collective social action for the collective social welfare. No appreciable number of citizens are willing to accept the total cost of higher education as they accept the cost of military preparedness or of the inspection of meat. The twentieth century has seen increasing acceptance of public responsibility for supporting state-controlled higher education, but the predominant folkways are still ones of viewing college education as a privilege accorded individuals, from which those individuals profit and for which those individuals—or some kind godfather—should pay.

The principle of distributing the total financial burden for operating education in proportion to ability to pay is not yet accepted at even the common school level. Equalization of burden within states is as yet not fully realized, and equalization between states is being bitterly contested in the United States Congress as this is written. The state as the fundamental unit of support for higher education is well established in the folkways, which is another way of saying that the principle of effort in terms of ability is not so established.

Unwillingness of the public to provide ready access to colleges and universities has accounted in large measure for a tradition that private philanthropy or religiously inspired donations should support an appreciable amount of higher education. This, combined with many other causes, has resulted in the evolution of a "system" of higher education composed of a mixture of state-controlled and privately controlled institutions. By tradition, tax support is confined to state-controlled institutions; to spend tax money through private agencies would, tradition says, violate the principle of separation of church and state and impose state control upon private enterprise.

Further, it is argued by some that increasing tax support for state-controlled colleges would constitute unfair competition to privately supported colleges and would mean the loss of many institutions that have rendered yeoman service in the past. Therefore, increased tax support is viewed with alarm and in some instances actually opposed on the grounds that it is an invasion of private rights.

The tradition that higher education is primarily a benefit to the individual has created a pattern of financial support that places considerable reliance upon student fees. Existence of fee support has blocked quite effectually the achievement of universal access to higher education and has contributed to unhealthy competition between colleges, but without such support at least one-fourth of the colleges and universities in the country would have to close their doors.

TRENDS IN SOURCES OF SUPPORT

Student Fees. The period between 1945 and 1949 saw a steady increase in the absolute amounts charged as fees to students, although latest available estimates indicate that the relative increase has not been equal to the decrease in the value of the dollar. In broad summary, the student fee is a major source of support only in private and church-related colleges, but in those institutions it appears to be absolutely vital.

Philanthropy. The proposition of total income for higher education derived from philanthropic sources has decreased steadily since 1919–20, although the gross amounts of annual contributions have increased appreciably.[3] It is estimated that in 1948–49 not more than 10 per cent of the edu-

[3] *Higher Education, Philanthropy, and Federal Tax Exemptions,* by Harold Goldthorpe (Washington: American Council on Education, and U. S. Office of Education, *Statistics of Higher Education,* p. 3).

cational expenditures of colleges and universities represented income from philanthropy. Certain other characteristics of philanthropic support should be noted: (1) Significant philanthropy is confined to a very few, mostly large, institutions; (2) while the quantity of philanthropy follows the national income, it has not increased in anything like direct proportion to that income; (3) the small givers, those with incomes under $5000, are accounting for more than 50 per cent of all philanthropy and the percentage is steadily increasing; (4) philanthropy has not followed the principle of equalizing educational opportunity; and (5) philanthropy is more and more directed to defraying current costs rather than to building up endowment funds.

Research Grants and Contracts. Once a minor consideration in financing higher education, annual research contracts and grants have now passed the 100-million mark, and bid fair to continue at such pace or go even higher. Such special research funds, as is the case with philanthropy, are largely concentrated in a few major institutions and do little to relieve the educational budgets of the recipient institutions.

Tax Funds. The spectacular financial news in the field of higher education is the decided upturn in appropriations made by legislatures and local tax bodies. Reports from 13 state legislatures meeting in 1949 indicate increases of from 25 to 45 per cent in the gross amounts appropriated for higher education. However, in no instance reported thus far has the increase in legislative appropriations since 1939–40 equalled the proportionate increase in student enrollment and the proportionate decrease in the purchasing power of the dollar. The slack has been taken up to some extent by federal appropriations for veterans' benefits, but no significant increase in federal grants for direct educational expenditures has occurred.

Hidden Sources. Although it never appeared on the balance sheet, the source of financial support that really kept most higher education going in prewar years was the donations by members of the faculties of colleges and universities. Those donations were in the form of unseen deductions from a living wage, or in other words, took the form of lowering salaries until the budget was balanced. Since 1940, average salaries have risen markedly in dollar value but, in general, are only slightly higher in purchasing power than were the salaries of 1939.

It is to these five sources, in the main, that the American public must go to secure financial support for a program of higher education that is fitted to the future. The utility of the sources themselves will have to be weighed in terms of democratic purposes. Even more important, the methods employed in tapping such sources should be conducive to the realization of democratic ideals.

Democratic Methods for Democratic Ends

Fees from Students? Access to higher education in a democracy can hardly be contingent upon the student's economic well-being. Neither can fees be justified on the ground of "he who benefits should pay." Presumably, the recipient of higher education pays for his personal profit later, through an ability-related system of taxation. Fees may have some justification as one imperfect substitute for taxes that cannot be enacted, but certainly their defects as tax-collecting devices are obvious.

What has been said of fees can be said with equal merit for the cost of living for students attending college. It would seem rather clear that a democratic society should move steadily away from individual assessment of students to pay for their education as potential leaders in American society.

In the interim, grants-in-aid will doubtless have to be employed freely to counteract the antidemocratic effects of money barriers to college attendance.

Philanthropy? At its best, philanthropy is an expression of brother-care-for-brother that is the foundationstone of democracy. With all its inefficiencies and short-sightedness, private philanthropy has in it some essence of the spirit of individualized and emotionalized good will that a society can hardly do without. It remains as one means of individual action for the good of the group. And, as Preacher Smith observed about a donation from a back-slidden gambler, "You can say it's tainted, but you can't say 'tain't money."

But in securing private gifts for higher education, what shall be the approach? Any concession for enough dollars? Cautious appeasement of those who control pursestrings? Abject apology for affronts to the sacred cows of the beneficent nobility? Fawning flattery and stomach-turning displays of obeisance before millions?

Or, a frank and skillful presentation of a cause to be served? An attempt to increase acceptance of social goals and high ideals? Appeals to the good sense of many little philanthropists? This latter route will not pay off in dollars so fast as the former in all likelihood. It seems, however, to be the only alternative for those who seek constructive philanthropy.

Faculty Donations? The tradition that college faculties can and should make up the difference between the money provided and the money needed will be hard to uproot. Many colleges will continue to exist in which the faculty member does in fact consider his time and energy as donations to a Cause, made without any desire for personal reward beyond the necessities of life. Such voluntary donations, however, are not the concern here. The concern is with a policy that consistently denies to a producer a reward commensurate with the value of what he produces. Higher education cannot meet the challenge of the future with underpaid, subjugated college faculty members. In the long run, society will get the service for which it pays.

More Tax Funds? It should be clear by now that the only hope for financial support of higher education in twentieth-century America lies in a sharp increase in tax funds. Students' fees can cushion the transition to new levels of service and private gifts can fill in some of the rough spots. However important these two sources may loom in an individual institution, they are only minor considerations in the total job to be done.

The tax-collecting power of the federal government should be called into play to produce a major share of the increased tax funds that are needed. It is not considered necessary here to repeat the clear-cut evidence that higher education is a national concern, a just charge against the national wealth. It becomes more and more apparent that state tax systems adequate to cope with the fluidity of modern wealth are hard to devise, leading inevitably to the adoption of the nation as one unit for school support.

State legislatures will continue, however, as the fundamental providers for higher education. Traditionally, higher education has approached legislatures for its appropriations—not the people who speak through legislators. It is doubtful that any old-fashioned political maneuvering with legislatures is going to be sufficient to get together the money that higher education needs. A new approach is indicated—an approach to the people themselves.

Pressure politics is seldom healthy for a democracy. Higher education has for too long staked its financial future on pressure politics. The new day calls for joining hands with the common school forces and taking the problems of education back to the people themselves, where they belong. Higher education is destined to be the people's education. Only they can determine its eventual nature. Only they can pay its eventual cost. The time to increase legislative appropriations is before the legislature is elected.

DISTRIBUTING FINANCIAL SUPPORT

America operates many colleges and universities already. Undoubtedly, it will operate more. Desirably, it will operate each one at peak efficiency in producing its own peculiar fruits for the benefit of democracy. Therefore, America must be concerned with how it distributes its funds for higher education among those institutions. It must be equally concerned with how each college or university allocates the funds thus placed at its disposal.

Between Public and Private Institutions. Distributing funds among colleges would be much simpler if all were either public or private. The dilemmas imposed by the coexistence of public education and private education seem to permeate every other consideration in deciding upon financial policy for higher education.

Dare America trust private colleges to serve the ends of higher education for American democracy? If so, it might well adopt the policy of providing for current educational expense in all colleges—through direct operation of public institutions and through tuition payments equal to per-student costs in public colleges for those persons who preferred a private college. Of course, private colleges would have to trust the public in return.

On the other hand, privately controlled colleges might be ignored in the distribution of tax funds. Strong institutions would continue to survive and would continue to attract financial support. Weaker institutions would vanish and, if they had been serving a genuinely useful purpose, public institutions would arise to replace them. The influence of strong private education would still be felt in the land, but how much the land would be weakened by the loss of private colleges unable to meet competition is moot. And, of course, the argument would not be silenced that when the state provides any education it acts as a usurper of the rights of the Church.

The important thing is that free access be provided to higher education for those who can profit society by receiving its benefits. It is antidemocratic to protect the proprietary interests of some at the expense of society as a whole. Expansion of public higher education need not be delayed until private higher education can keep pace. If the alleged unique contributions of private colleges are needed, and the need is recognized by the people of America, resources are available for paying the cost of those colleges. The small additional tax burden imposed on potential donors by expanded public higher education can hardly be considered as a real deterrent to the support of private institutions. These and other considerations lead, therefore, to the proposition that tax funds should be distributed only to publicly controlled institutions, whether by direct payments or by grants-in-aid to students.

Between the States. Without elaboration it may be stated that the distribution of tax funds between the states should achieve equalization of educational opportunity. Opportunity, of course, is interpreted in terms of the accessibility of a minimum level of educational service, and will include cost of living as well as cost of operation. Surely the equalization principle has been documented beyond all argument. Emotion and tradition constitute the only barriers to its acceptance; those barriers must be removed.

Within a State. Very few states have anything that could be termed a *system* of higher education. Individual units have grown up, largely without any conception of a master plan or of coordinated expenditure of effort. Wasteful duplications are common; even more wasteful lack of comprehensiveness is often apparent. All too frequently, the available financial support from public funds is parceled out in proportion to political pressure.

Within the past two decades, however, more and more coordination has been achieved in planning for public higher education within states. Over-all budgets, or at least mutually approved budgets, are being submitted to legislatures. Some progress has been made in developing objective formulas for the allocation of support. These and similar movements in the direction of increased coordination are to be highly commended; their pace should be accelerated.

One barrier to the proper distribution of public funds for the support of higher education within a state lies in the traditional hierarchy of institutions. The state university, usually the oldest, has established one expenditure level. Other general-purpose colleges have been assigned another, usually lower. Ex-normal schools, now regional general-purpose colleges, have still a third. Separate Negro colleges, if they exist, have a fourth. Yet each college provides for its students most of the higher education those students will ever get. Differences in expenditures if they reflect differences in minimum quality are hard to justify.

In brief, then, distribution of support funds within a state should be designed to buy the people the very most possible for their money. Such purchasing is a technical job, requiring the services of permanent, technically trained personnel directed by policies established by the people themselves.

Within an Institution. In the final analysis, the productiveness of America's investment in higher education depends upon the objects of expenditure adopted by individual colleges and universities. Within the limits imposed upon this discussion, only a few pertinent considerations can be treated. They will be considerations which call for decided budgetary reorientation by most institutions.

A prime function of higher education is to make the most of the human resources with which it deals. Resources undiscovered, resources undeveloped, resources unreleased—these are wasted resources. To discover human resources, much money must be spent on psychological and analytic services. To develop resources, much money must be spent on teachers and teaching equipment, and still more money on improving the teaching processes. To release resources, money must be spent on counseling and clinical services, on remedial activities, on inspirational opportunities. Current budgets give small emphasis to the resource-development functions of higher education.

Call it citizenship education or general education—the core of justification for colleges and universities of the future will be found in what they do to equip people with the skills of living. One university spends more annually on providing medical education for 240 students than it spends to provide general education for 12,000 students. The expense for medical education may be justified, but the low expenditure for general education is indefensible.

Budgets also have much to do with research accomplishments. The allocation of truly significant amounts to research in the sciences of human behavior is one much-to-be-desired earmark of an institution that is distributing its local funds with social conscience.

Then, finally, one somewhat selfish plea. Colleges and universities have the privilege of being the first training ground of those who will teach in schools and colleges. Through the years, professional education for teachers has been operated on an extremely meager basis. More money could turn out immeasurably better teachers, an essential ingredient of an effective democracy. Local fiscal policy may thus become enlightened social policy.

In Conclusion

Much has been left unsaid about the financial side of operating higher education in the American democracy. What has been said reemphasizes the point of view that money spent for higher education is, in effect, the accumulation of social capital from which interest may be expected in direct proportion to the amount invested. The methods by which the original investment is accumulated and expended determine in large measure the productivity of the social capital that is built up.

CHAPTER XII

STUDYING THE STUDENTS
AND THEIR COMMUNITIES

HAROLD C. HAND

University of Illinois

BY VIRTUE of the central value it strives to embody, a democratic society places a heavy responsibility upon its institutions of higher learning in reference to the diagnosis of students. As the President's Commission on Higher Education has succinctly observed,[1] "The fundamental concept of democracy is a belief in the inherent worth of the individual, in the dignity and value of human life." The Commission has remarked earlier, "The first goal in education for democracy is the full, rounded, and continuing development of the person. . . . To liberate and perfect the intrinsic powers of every citizen is the central purpose of democracy, and its furtherance of individual self-realization is its greatest glory." [2]

Not only, says the Commission, will education ". . . necessarily vary its means and methods to fit the diversity of its

[1] President's Commission on Higher Education, *Higher Education for American Democracy*, Vol. I, p. 11 (Washington: U. S. Government Printing Office, 1947).
[2] *Ibid.*, p. 9.

constituency, but it will achieve its ends more successfully if its programs and policies grow out of and are relevant to the characteristics and needs of contemporary society. Effective democratic education will deal directly with current problems." [3] If they are effectively to discharge the social responsibility here so clearly implied, it is apparent that a continuing diagnosis of the social scene must be made by the colleges and universities.

The purpose of this chapter is to make more explicit the character of these two interrelated responsibilities. As fully as limitations of space will permit, we shall attempt to detail the specific things about its students and their communities that our institutions of higher learning should continuously be appraising. We shall deal first with the study of students.

Studying the Students

Since the "full, rounded, and continuing development of the person" clearly means "from the eyebrows both ways," the number of things that the college needs to know about its students is anything but inconsiderable. Parenthetically, the author knows of but few institutions in which more than a scarcely respectable fraction of the obviously necessary types of data about to be noted are systematically secured and utilized.

Physiological Data. The first items to which attention will be directed are principally physiological in character. Providing for the health of its students is an important objective of an institution of higher learning. The health status of the student is a basic determinant of most if not all of the other types of development which colleges and universities should seek to engender. The test questions here suggested include the following: Is there an accurate and reasonably inclusive

[3] *Ibid.*, pp. 5–6.

periodic check-up of the health status of each student? If remedial or preventive action is indicated, is there systematic provision for seeing to it that such action is taken? If a student has defective vision, are adequate steps taken to remedy the situation if the condition is correctable? If it is not, is the student's environment (special lighting, special seating, special instructional materials and methods) so arranged and supervised that his deficiency is minimized? If he has a serious hearing loss, are appropriate steps (special seating, hearing aids, lip-reading instruction) taken to overcome the difficulty to the degree that it is possible? If students are variously in need of medication, surgery, dental care, a special diet, does the administration somehow see to it that these are had? If the energy output of a student is low, or if he has a cardiac or other debilitating condition, does his total program reflect an adequate consideration of this fact? Are communicable diseases as effectively controlled as possible within the college community? Is each professor or other staff member specifically and regularly advised of the special status of each student in his classes or under his charge whose welfare requires that one or more special provisions be made for him? More than this, is there some systematic procedure for checking up to see to it that these special provisions are as fully as possible made?

If our institutions were to be appraised on the basis of the questions just noted, it is doubtful that more than a scattered few would score higher than about 10 on a 100-point scale. Here, apparently, is an item of unfinished business the magnitude of which clearly shows that we have gone only a small part of the way in providing for the "full, rounded, and continuing development" of our students in a physiological sense.

Mental Health Data. The emotional no less than the physical health status of a student is, in addition to being in and of itself a basically important aspect of development, an important determinant of the extent to which the other objectives of the college will be achieved. Consequently, the institution should know each of its students in this as fully as it does in a physical health sense. Too frequently, it is only the extreme deviants (the "problem" cases) among the student body who are thus appraised in any thoroughgoing way. Since all professors and other staff members who shape the experiences of students in any way either aid or hinder their emotional development, it is apparent that the pertinent facts in this regard about each student should so far as is possible or wise be made known to these staff members. Included among the descriptive items which should thus be put to work are those relating to the emotional stability of the student, the nature and probable causes of any noteworthy difficulties or deficiencies he may typify, and an indication of whatever special needs he may have. All that is pertinent in these and related respects should be known by and acted upon by the clinically trained counselors on the staff. Some of this information is helpful to the general faculty in aiding them in providing an environment more conducive to good emotional health. Provided only that its intelligent utilization does not require special competencies not ordinarily possessed by them, all such information should systematically be made available to the members of the faculty. If necessary (and it usually is) the teaching corps should be instructed by the clinical staff in reference to the intelligent utilization of such data.

As matters now stand, very seldom does one find a college or university in which there are enough clinically trained counselors to work with even the relatively small number of more or less extreme deviants, to say nothing of the general student body. Extremely rare is the institution in which an instructor is regularly supplied with any information whatsoever about his students in addition to their names, class designation, and possibly one or two similar "bookkeeping" items. Rare, too, is the college or university in which classes are small enough to permit instructors to utilize personal data if they were supplied. Effective personal attention to students and mass education simply do not go together.

Academic Aptitude Data. This brings us to a third type of information about students which the college or university should secure. Happily, it is one that virtually all institutions do get and, with varying degrees of wisdom, use. Reference here is to measures of the students' academic aptitudes as revealed by so-called intelligence tests. Although the validity of these instruments is open to serious question when used to appraise students from the lower socio-economic groups,[4] the data they ordinarily yield are indispensable in rounding out the clinical picture of a student. The clinically trained counselor is quite unlikely to be misled, or to mislead others, by intelligence test data. He knows the inherent limitations of these appraisal devices. Equally important, he knows that what we call intelligence is but one of several important things that must be known about a student before the student can be described in any reasonably accurate sense that is meaningful within the context of what a college or university should be attempting to do through, with, or to its students. In the hands of an improperly trained or untrained person, however, intelligence test data may be, and usually are, used unwisely at best. At worst, these test data when so utilized figure in a species of unwitting charlatanism which is vicious in its consequences.

Communication Skills Data. The students' communication skills constitute a fourth important determinant of college success. The engendering of these skills is also central among

---

[4] "Schools and the Lower Socio-Economic Groups," by Allison Davis (*Education Digest*, Vol. 14, February, 1949, pp. 1-4).

the objectives of democratic education. It follows, then, that the college should have an accurate appraisal of each student's rate of reading, level of reading comprehension, skill in written expression, skill in oral expression, and ability to listen with understanding and discrimination. The needs of each student in reference to each of these communication skills should be carefully and periodically diagnosed, and the resultant data (preferably accompanied by helpful recommendations for remediation or further developement) systematically transmitted to the student's current instructors and advisers. Whether or not he is aware of the fact, every instructor is either a help or a hindrance to his students in reference to the development of these skills. This is true in all subjects, in all extra-class activities, and in all other situations involving communication in any form. By the examples he sets, the methods he employs, and the standards he expects or requires in reference to whatever media of communication his subject or activity entails, each faculty member inevitably either helps or hinders the development of students in this important regard.

At the present, only the student's reading test data are more or less commonly a matter of record; only in rare instances are the other communication skills systematically appraised. Even among that probable majority of colleges and universities in which reading tests are regularly administered, however, the resultant data are but very seldom communicated in any systematic way to the teaching staff. The generality of American colleges and universities has yet to demonstrate that the communication skills are being accorded the careful and continuous attention which their importance in a democracy clearly warrants. Not only must its members communicate adequately in order to make democracy work; the skills of communication also constitute a basic requisite for effective self-realization.

Reflective Thinking Data. Since democracy is based upon the appeal to reason, and since "straight thinking" is a basic ingredient of sound reasoning, we have here a fifth important category of information about its students which institutions of higher learning should secure and utilize. Although useful tests of many of the special abilities which go to make up straight thinking have been available for some time, and have for some years been utilized by our better secondary schools, relatively few colleges and universities have as yet exploited them. Since every subject in the curriculum is supposed to teach straight thinking, it is apparent that every instructor should know with what "given" in regard to this ability he is confronted when he faces a new class. Obviously, the collecting of such test data at periodic intervals and its systematic distribution to every member of the teaching staff would appreciably facilitate the achieving of this important institutional objective.

Occupational Aptitude Data. A sixth type of needed information is suggested by the fact that the democratically adequate man or woman will, among other things, be competent to earn a living in an occupation well suited to his interests and abilities which he has chosen on the basis of intelligent self-direction. As every competent vocational counselor knows, there are standardized inventories, scales, and tests which are of great value to students in assessing their occupational interests, capacities, and abilities. These counselors also know that a record of the student's past successes and failures (or likes and dislikes) in school subjects, extra-class activities, work experiences, and leisure-time pursuits is significantly revealing in these respects. Consequently, such instruments will be utilized and such records will be gathered and put to work by colleges and universities that are genuinely dedicated to the "full, well-rounded, and continuing development" of their students. A sizeable minority of American collegiate institutions has developed very commendable programs in this regard.

Social Skills Data. In any society such as ours in which the "furtherance of individual self-realization is its greatest glory," the development of social skills should be an important educational objective. The social skills which are requisite or desirable in such a society go far beyond the skills of communication to which reference has already been made. Included here would be the development of social sensitivity, skill in making and keeping friends, skill in meeting people, skill in grooming, conversational skill, skill in conducting a wholesome courtship and in selecting a suitable mate, skill in managing a home and in rearing children intelligently, and skill in participating in at least some of a whole host of recreational and cultural pursuits. Diagnoses and evaluations of the types just indicated would be made by any institution seriously concerned with the development of such skills, and the resultant data would be put to work in the service of improving the guidance and instruction of its students in the respects noted.

The fact that so few institutions of higher learning solicit such information about students suggests that they do not regard the development of social skills as an important objective. If they do regard it as important, it is evident that they are willing to proceed without benefit of diagnosis as to student need or appraisal of student progress. Neither interpretation can be regarded as flattering.

Data on Skills in Democratic Participation. Still another major characteristic of American social philosophy dictates an eighth type of diagnostic and evaluative data. For all its citizens, our society postultes democratic participation in shaping the total life of the community. This clearly requires that the skills essential to such participation be learned, hence implies that they be taught in the schools and collegiate institutions. Prominent among the abilities requisite to democratic participation are skill in working cooperatvely with others, skill in criticizng tactfully and differing peaceably, skill in influencing public opinion in socially desirable ways, skill in abiding by majority decisions in a sportsman-like way, skill in selecting wise leadership, skill in leading without dominating, skill in using freedom intelligently with a due regard for the rights and feelings of others, and skill in establishing a self-imposed type of law and order conducive to the greatest good to the greatest number and favorable to the greatest possible realization of all the other values of democracy.

As previously noted, it is of the essence of education for democracy that these and kindred skills be taught, and well taught. Consequently, it is important that the development of students in these vitally necessary respects be adequately diagnosed and appraised. Virtually no institution systematically secures and utilizes such information about the members of its student body. This is serious in the extreme, for the "good democrat" is not "born"; he must be created. This can be done only through education—more importantly, only through the kind of education which is pointedly designed for this purpose. The type of development here connoted is too vitally important to be left to guesswork.

Data on Values, Beliefs, and Attitudes. We come now to a ninth type of information about students which should be secured and used as a basis for guidance and instruction. The category here recommended is basic to all democratic behavior; it is that category inclusive of the values, beliefs, and attitudes of the learners. The principal diagnostic and evaluative items that are needed in this regard can perhaps best be suggested in question form. Does the student believe that human life, happiness, and well-being are to be valued above all else? Is he convinced that *all* human beings are of supreme (hence equivalent) moral worth, or does he make invidious distinctions among the various racial, religious, socio-economic, national, or other groups? Does he believe in full equality of opportunity? Does he have faith in human intelligence and in the appeal to reason; does he believe that man is architect of his own destiny, and that by taking thought he can build a better world? Is he convinced of the necessity of safeguarding freedom of belief, inquiry, expression, and association? Is he persuaded that men are entitled to freedom from want, fear, and ignorance? Does he believe that the right to work must be guaranteed? Is he committed to majority rule, but with the full protection of minorities? Is he convinced that prosperity and peace are respectively indivisible? Does he believe that world government based on world law is now an imperative, and that world peace and global well-being can be secured only on the basis of the "intellectual and moral union of mankind"? Is he appropriately sensitive to cultural differences; does he regard these as normal and reasonable developments carrying potential enrichment values for other cultures, or does he assume that such differences imply an innate inferiority—on the other fellow's part, of course? Does he regard himself as a citizen of the world, with the welfare of everybody everywhere his proper concern? In short, what and how much of the "value stuff" that is requisite for good citizenship in our time does the student bring to whatever the course or extra-class activity may be?

Scales and inventories designed to appraise a student's status in regard to some of the attitudes just noted are now available. Regrettably, however, they are not generally utilized by colleges and universities. If these attitudes are important enough to teach, they are important enough to diagnose and appraise. It is to be hoped that instruments useful for purposes of diagnosing and evaluating over the full range of socially significant attitudes will be developed and that these will come into general use. Education in reference to values is certainly too important to be permitted to remain in the realm of guesswork.

Subject Matter Data. The fact that certain institutional objectives will in substantial part be achieved through subject matter implies another species of diagnostic and evaluative evidence about students that facilitates good teaching. Reference here is to those among the standardized tests of subject matter which are valid measures of important content. This usage is so well-known that no further mention of it will be made here.

Student Appraisal Data. The eleventh and last category of information about students to be approvingly indicated has to do with what the recipients of our instruction think about their courses and their instructors. It is our view that students should always be privileged and expected to submit at their conclusion an appraisal of the courses they have taken. If the right sort of human relations obtains, there is no need for providing the safeguard of anonymity; for, by definition, no safeguard of this or any other sort would be either needed or desired in such situations. As matters now stand on most campuses, however, it is highly probable that this safeguard would not only be desired by the students but that it would have to be provided if frank and honest appraisals are to be had. The instrument used for this purpose should be designed to elicit the students' opinions of every feature and aspect of the course, the behavior of the instructor included. No instructor who is sincerely desirous of improving the nature and quality of the experiences which students have under his guidance will shrink from this proposal; on the contrary, it will be welcomed by such individuals.

A careful inquiry would probably reveal that this appraisal procedure is but very rarely employed in our colleges and universities. Instead, it would appear that students are typically required to "take it and like it." This is neither democracy in education nor good education for democracy.

One further comment regarding students' appraisals of their courses and of their instructors is in order. It is that this procedure can be—and in some cases has been—abused by administrators not genuinely dedicated to democracy. If used only to insure a fuller and more frank species of communication between students and professor, it is to be highly recommended. It (and any and all persons who so employ it) is to be damned, however, if utilized for purposes of spying.

Studying the Communities

Now that we have noted what are probably the major types of information about students which should be secured, we turn to a consideration of the obligations of the college or university to study the communities they serve. We shall first suggest the framework within which these considerations will be presented.

There are certain basic social processes which must adequately be carried on if societal good health is to be had. It can easily be demonstrated that the successful carrying forward of any and all of these basic social processes requires *learned behavior*; that each requires that the population must *understand*, *believe*, and *do* certain things rather than their opposites; hence that the effective discharge of any and all such survival imperatives is a function of education. That only artifacts remain to remind us of some of the world's once great cultures attests the antecedent fact that their educational "systems" were inadequate to the operational demands of these necessary processes. As New Fist could testify, what the bearers of these now defunct cultures needed to *know*, *believe*, and *do* in order to insure societal survival was *not* effectively educated into their nervous systems. The societal consequence of such educational inadequacies, now and in the future as well as then, is inevitably a regression through stagnation and decay to ultimate liquidation. These basic social processes, then, provide a valid framework for outlining the community study responsibilities of our institutions of higher learning.

Vocational Data. One of these essential processes has to do with vocational education. If it is to remain (or become) strong, any society must enable its population to make a living. Clearly, the institutions of higher learning have an obligation to provide both vocational guidance and vocational education. Neither can effectively be done except as the college or university grounds its program in the actual present and probable future facts of the occupational world. Here, then, is suggested one type of societal study which is requisite to any effective collegiate education which looks to the "full, rounded, and continuing development" of the student.

Data on World Cultures. If it is to escape commitment to the wastebasket of history, any society in whatever time or place must successfully provide physical security for its members. In our time, in addition to providing internal security, this means guaranteeing world peace. Obviously, this will require "community" study on a world-wide scale if valid guides to effective education for peace are to be had. To date, this type of community study has been almost entirely restricted to a certain few of the countries of the West. The cultures of Asia, Africa, and South America must now be similarly studied.

Health Data. A third imperative for societal strength is that the population be kept healthy and vigorous and that it be safeguarded against accidents and disease. Since behavior is the only certain test of education, collegiate institutions should note how adequately or inadequately this essential social process is being carried on in the communities it serves. On the basis of the resultant data, a determination should be made of what should be taught to those who are destined to be the leaders in these communities.

Natural Resources Data. Nothing contributes more certainly or inexorably to societal stagnation and decay than the neglecting of natural resources. If societal good health is to be had, the population must develop, wisely utilize, and conserve its basic biotic and physical resources. If it is to be done, its leaders must obviously be educated accordingly. The record in America to date clearly proves that our community leaders have not been so prepared. Here, then, is another aspect of community study which colleges and universities can neglect only at a ghastly cost to the communities they are supposed to be serving.

Child Rearing Data. To be strong, any society must appropriately rear and educate its young. Millions of America's future citizens are today being miserably reared and inadequately educated. Given our professed aspirations, our national wealth, and the status of our technical "know-how," this must be regarded as a national disgrace as well as a serious threat to our future. Obviously, since performance is the test of education, our community leaders have not been adequately educated. Much more community study in reference to this social process is clearly indicated for our colleges and universities if their programs are to prove adequate to the need.

Esthetic and Spiritual Data. Enabling the population to satisfy its esthetic and spiritual impulses is still another social process for which adequate educational provision must be made. No competent, unbiased, and honest observer could appraise the generality of Americans and of American communities and assert that enough adequately trained leaders in reference to this aspect of living have yet been supplied.

It is not unlikely that most collegiate faculty members have but a partial knowledge of what the "given" is in this regard in the generality of the communities served by their respective institutions. This aspect of community study is another which appears to require considerable strengthening.

Leisure Time Data. How the population spends its leisure time is the subject matter of another of the social processes to which the institutions of higher learning should be sensitive. Since a people improperly educated in reference to avocational tastes and skills is invariably a bored aggregate, and since escape from boredom is so generally sought in activities that are personally destructive and/or socially disintegrative, it is apparent that adequate community leadership in respect to recreational life is a requisite for societal good health. Every recognized authority in the field of leisure and recreation seems to agree that our communities are typically starved for leadership in this area. Apparently, much more community study of this facet of American life is required of our colleges and universities.

Values Data. If it is to constitute a unified whole, any culture group must be bound together by a body of commonly held beliefs and aspirations. Consequently, the engendering of such a commonly held system of values is obviously an essential social process. For America, this social cement is afforded by the values of democracy. Nothing, it would seem, could be more important for a college or university to know than how these values fare in the communities it serves.

Governing Data. Last in the list of basic social processes is that which has to do with governing. Obviously, if it is to have the strength that only integration can afford, any society must have its population so organized and governed that all the other processes will successfully be carried forward in consonance with its commonly held beliefs and aspirations. Unless it knows how the communities it seeks to serve are organized and governed, an institution of higher learning can scarecely know either the character or the extent of the needs which it should be meeting in this important regard. Obviously, this inclusive type of community study is one requisite basis for an effective program of democratic education.

We come now to a brief concluding statement. This chapter has argued that the central values of democracy dictate that colleges and universities must in certain named ways diagnose both the students and the communities they are attempting to serve. The inevitable alternative to adequate diagnosis is that of proceeding on the basis of guesswork. Education for democracy is too crucially important to be permitted to remain in this dimly lighted realm.

CHAPTER XIII

SELECTING AND DEVELOPING
APPROPRIATE INSTITUTIONAL ACTIVITIES

R. LEE HORNBAKE

University of Maryland

THE same forces which give structure to institutional objectives determine also the activities which shall be pursued in the advancement of those objectives. Stated differently, the objectives may be regarded as the generalizations about which the institutional activities are classified and synthesized.

The budget, the formal statement of objectives, and the policies pertaining to the selection and placement of personnel are phases of institutional operation which may be kept within the complete jurisdiction of a few people. The harmful effects of authoritarian control over these matters have been explained in Chapters IV and VIII. Nevertheless there are those faculty members, trustees, administrators, and others who will continue to regard the above-mentioned operations as belonging rightfully to *the* administration. But the ongoing program of the institution provides inescapable points of contact with all faculty members, all students, all parents, all alumni, and all those who offer financial support.

There is no chronic indifference to the activities engaged in by higher education. The opinions, beliefs, and values of people are expressed in terms of what a school ought to do, or ought not to do; what it should emphasize, or deemphasize. The value may be crystallized in the form of a request for a winning football team, for research directed toward improving the blueberry crop of a state, for the maintenance of a chair in Latin, for an off-campus course serving a management group in a local industry. Opinions relevant to institutional activities may be expressed through the press, or in legislative halls, or in reports of investigative or accrediting committees, or from the platform of a national convention of a pressure group. A given institution is appraised by individuals and by groups in terms of the activities conducted and, primarily, in terms of the activities with which the appraiser identifies himself. There is the normal tendency for an institution to move in the direction of the pressures which are applied. This condition led Bode[1] to conclude: "The basic trouble with the modern college is that, like Stephen Leacock's horsemen, it rides off in all directions at once."

Many different appraisals are naturally made of the same institution. Evaluations are made by students, school patrons, friends and opponents, and also by professional staff members. Democratic administration will keep open the channels whereby these differences may be expressed and given due regard. Democratic administration will also continually point up those fundamental issues on which decisions should be reached even though such issues may be obscured by less important, time-consuming considerations. That is, good administration will take the initiative in placing matters of primary importance at the top of the agenda.

[1] "The Confusion in Present-Day Education," by Boyd H. Bode, in *The Educational Frontier*, pp. 15–16, William H. Kilpatrick, editor (New York: The Century Co., 1933).

CONSIDERATIONS BASIC TO DETERMINING INSTITUTIONAL ACTIVITIES

Several of the persistent problems which confront higher education and which influence the institutional activities are presented.

Clarifying the Purposes of Education in American Democracy. Chapter I has been devoted to this topic and supplementary comments appear in Chapter II and XII. However, purpose or social function is so fundamental to the procedure of determining activities that it merits restatement. The usual fragmentizing of higher education into curricula and subjects, the perennial financial crises, and the diverse expectations held by students, parents, donors, and taxpayers narrow the perspective and may result in a neglect to note that higher education has an exacting social responsibility. The same conditions lead to a neglect of the individual student. Since, in a democracy, the ultimate purpose of education is the optimum growth of the individual, the neglect of social purpose and the neglect of individuality are two ways of saying the same thing.

To attempt a comprehensive statement of the purpose of higher education in American democracy would be much too lengthy for inclusion at this point. Something in the way of a summarizing statement is to be found in the Report of the President's Commission on Higher Education.[2] It reads:

. . . . Thus the social role of education in a democratic society is at once to insure equal liberty and equal opportunity to differing individuals and groups, and to enable the citizens to understand, appraise, and redirect forces, men, and events as these tend to strengthen or to weaken their liberties.

In performing this role, education will necessarily vary its means and methods to fit the diversity of its constituency, but it will achieve

[2] President's Commission on Higher Education. *Higher Education for American Democracy.* Vol. 1. Establishing the Goals, pp. 5–6 (Washington, D. C.: U. S. Government Printing Office, 1947).

its ends more successfully if its program and policies grow out of and are kept relevant to the characteristics and needs of contemporary society. Effective democratic education will deal directly with current problems.

. . . . At the same time education is the making of the future. Its role in a democratic society is that of critic and leader as well as servant; its task is not merely to meet the demands of the present but to alter those demands if necessary, so as to keep them always suited to democratic ideals. Perhaps its most important role is to serve as an instrument of social transition, and its responsibilities are defined in terms of the kind of civilization society hopes to build. . . .

The above is, of course, a broad statement of purpose. The responsibility of administration is to implement the statement. This, too, is very general. It is significant, though, to note that two important factors in its pursuit are the qualities of human relationships which are engendered in the school community and the selection of learning experiences. While finances are essential to the institutional life, neither favorable human relations nor the techniques of selecting proper learning experiences are purchasable items.

Defining the Institution's Area of Operation. The charter or constitution of an institution sets forth the purposes of the school and the types of services it may render. As is true of most corporation charters this very general declaration is subject to interpretation. Interpretation should be a continual process not in the manner of taking on new shades of meaning for purposes of "empire building" but rather in the sense of *refinement* so that the integrity of the institution may be maintained. There is nothing more dissipating of institutional energy than the policy of opportunism wherein the school endeavors to exploit every promising area of operation, regardless of the tangents which may result.

There are countless occasions when the institutional purpose needs to be reviewed. The development of new colleges within a university, the opening of new departments within colleges, the adding of new courses within departments, as well as their counterparts in the way of terminations or deletions, are instances where decisions should not rest primarily upon the intrinsic quality of the plan. Instead, appraisals should be based upon pertinence to the goals of the institution.

The intent of referring decisions to "What is our reason for being?" does not preclude new developments or additional services. It does provide a frame of reference for deciding whether the proposal implements or contradicts major institutional goals. Democratic administration will endeavor to get a maximum of participation in this evaluation so that decisions may rest upon a broad base of understanding.

Higher education is comprised of a variety of institutions. Collectively considered they can be most instrumental in advancing the democratic way of life not by broadening their scope so that each becomes like the other but rather through having each carry out its specific functions to the optimum of its capacity. Institutions, like people, should develop individuality; they should strive for distinctiveness.

Resolving Educational Issues. Higher education, dealing with mature minds, is the level at which educational issues are most keenly pointed. It is here that the relative emphasis merited by general and vocational education is warmly debated; it is here that other philosophical questions of origins of truth, nature of experience, and concepts of mind make for sharp differences of opinion. It is only natural for these differences to prevail and it is a commendable circumstance when there is sufficient intellectual vigor to make for fair discussion of these differences. It is tragic when the several schools of thought set themselves apart in tight compartments and resist compromise. The student is then the likely victim of these factions and he must practice duplicity in his endeavor to satisfy the conflicting demands made of him.

The function of democratic administration is to provide ways and means of intercommunication among persons, departments, and colleges where varying viewpoints prevail. It should not be expected that *all* differences are to be reconciled either at the outset or at any time in the future. Initial agreements may be on minor points only but, if so, then the implementation of these minor agreements provides the hope for more consequential developments. But at all times the administration should insure an atmosphere which permits the student to grow and develop without having to align himself with one faction or another in order to gain academic security.

Administration should provide the leadership essential to honest decisions on these fundamental, philosophical matters. There is perhaps no area of institutional activity in which the thinking is looser than in the instance of general education. General, cultural, or liberal education has come to be associated with a series of courses in the social sciences, humanities, and mathematics. Each of the courses tends to be oriented about some principle which inheres within the discipline, despite high-sounding claims for informed, responsible life in a democratic society via general education.

An example of apparent inconsistency in this regard appears in the Harvard Report. A statement[3] is made early in the Report that: ". . . . a general education is distinguished from special education, not by subject matter, but in terms of method and outlook, no matter what the field. . . ." Later in the Report consideration is given to less gifted or inept students who have difficulty with abstract mathematics and who must be presented with mathematics in "various disguises" such as shop mathematics, business arithmetic, and the like. At this point the Committee concludes:[4]

[3] Harvard Report (Report of the Harvard Committee), *General Education in a Free Society*, p. 56 (Cambridge: Harvard University Press, 1945).
[4] *Ibid.*, p. 164. (Italics in the original.)

. . . . In such an approach, however, one has been forced to concede one of the primary values of mathematics instruction in general education. Mathematics comprises both abstraction and the application of the results obtained by abstraction to specific real problems. Of these aspects, the basic one is abstraction. Only because it is abstract is mathematics applicable generally to problems which arise in widely different areas. When a student has reached his limit of tolerance in handling abstractions, his *general* education in mathematics must also come to an end.

Hêre, then, is a clear-cut suggestion of an organizing principle for general education. The "true" principle for selecting general education mathematics turns out to be *abstraction* and since all normal persons are not capable of dealing with abstractions, as defined, their general education in mathematics must come to an end. What promised to be an education for all and directed toward responsible citizenship came to grief on the principle of abstraction. Even general education must perforce become an esoteric education if this line of reasoning is accepted.

Others have suggested overarching principles for general education such as the pursuit of "first and ultimate truths." It is not obvious how these eternal truths are revealed nor how they are guaranteed. But once reached the implication is that they transcend empirical observation and hence cannot be tested in ordinary experience. This avenue to general, liberal, or cultural education makes higher education a mythological affair devoid of human values and human relationships. These are but two of the many suggestions made for determining the program of general education.

Any proposal should be examined systematically for the assumptions involved, for the evidence offered in support of claims made, and for the genesis of the idea. The history of education reveals instances where educational practices have been continued for reasons invented and invoked when the conditions which gave rise to the practice ceased to exist. On this point Beard has said:[5]

> Once created and systematized, any program of educational thought and practice takes on professional and institutional stereotypes, and tends to outlast even profound changes in the society in which it assumed its original shape.

The consistency of thought which democratic administration can encourage emanates from the hypothesis that democracy requires an indigenous education, general or otherwise. If general education is to refer specifically to the skills, understandings, and values which are needed by all persons living in a democratic society, then these skills, understandings, and values are to be found in democratic living. Thus considered, democratic administration is not simply a composite of methods; it is as much the development of an educational program which advances the democratic way of life.

Implementing Instructional Objectives. The problem of relating instruction to educational objectives is of long standing. Plato showed regard for it as he discussed in the *Republic* the requirements of the warrior guardian. As soon as it was agreed that the warrior guardian should unite in himself "philosophy and spirit and swiftness and strength"[6] Plato said, "Then we have found the desired natures; and now that we have found them, how are they to be reared and educated?"[7] It was agreed that the educational plan should consist of gymnastics for the body and music, including literature, for the soul. But not just any literature was good for the purpose. In fact, some tales were known to be contradictory to the desired ends. To preclude the use of "wrong" litera-

[5] National Education Association (Educational Policies Commission). *The Unique Function of Education in American Democracy*, p. 6 (Washington, D. C.: The Association, 1937).

[6] *The Republic of Plato*, p. 56. Translated by Benjamin Jowett (New York: Wiley Book Company, 1901).

[7] *Ibid.*, p. 56.

ture Plato proposed a censorship of the writers of fiction and only "authorized" literature was to be used.

Plato, in his concern for the education of such a specific calling as the warrior guardian in a class-structured society, acknowledged the importance of first defining educational goals in terms of *human behavior*. Higher education has neglected the cue offered by Plato. Only infrequently have we raised the question: What behavior changes do we expect to make in these people? Much more generally we have thought in terms of subject matter, of required subjects, of credits, and of degrees. General and catchy statements of pious hopes are of little assistance in determining instructional content and method. Instead, what is needed is a series of "plumbers' English" statements describing how a person with a baccalaureate or doctorate degree will change his behavioral patterns in the process of earning a degree, and the kind of person he will be. This does not lead necessarily to a stereotyping of the educational product. It does mean that in order for higher education to operate above the level of intuition and mysticism, it must know what types of behavior it champions.

But reality in instructional goals requires much more than the breakdown of objectives in terms of human behavior. There is need also for selecting experiences which are likely to produce the changes desired. Prerequisites to these choices are (1) an understanding of the learner and (2) knowledge of the learning process. In these regards higher education has a long road to travel. As an example, higher education has been most naive in its concept of transfer of learning. One very prevalent learning assumption in higher education has been tested by Tyler[8] in a series of studies involving eleven

[8] "The Relation Between Recall and Higher Mental Processes," by Ralph W. Tyler, in *Education as Cultivation of the Higher Mental Processes*, pp. 6–18 (New York: The Macmillan Co., 1936).

subject fields. Tyler learned through interviews that 60 per cent of the students in college believed

> . . . . the chief duty of college students is to memorize the information which instructors consider important. . . . The vast majority of examinations mainly require students to remember and state facts presented in textbooks and lectures. It is not surprising that students think of memorization as the fundamental requirement in education.[9]

Tyler also generalized that:

> Many instructors who recognized this prevalent attitude among students do not decry it but consider it a satisfactory stimulus to study. They hold that study regardless of its emphasis will result in the development of facility in reflective thinking. . . .[10]

Devices were developed to determine the relationships between the ability to recall information and (1) the ability to recall principles taught and to apply them to new situations, and (2) the ability to draw reasonable inferences from data that had not been presented to the students before. Coefficients of correlation were computed for the relationships existing between items (1) and (2) as well.

The coefficients of correlation were uniformly low. Most of the corrected for attenuation values were between .35 and .45. Tyler's concluding statement was:

> . . . . It is shown that a large number of students studying a variety of subjects did not develop corresponding degrees of facility in mere recall and facility in the higher mental processes of applying principles and drawing inferences. Memorization of facts frequently fails to result in the development of higher mental processes. If the higher mental processes of application of principles and inference are really to be cultivated, learning conditions appropriate for their cultivation are necessary.[11]

Professional people employed in higher education have

[9] *Ibid.,* p. 6.
[10] *Ibid.,* p. 6.
[11] *Ibid.,* pp. 16–17.

greatly diverse backgrounds. They are frequently chosen for their expertness in a subject field. An instructor may be an authority and on the frontier in his field of economics, or botany, or mathematics yet have only the most archaic notions of the learning process. His professional preparation may have been entirely void of experiences relevant to human growth and development. Democratic administration will not be able to overcome this handicap simply by requiring an applicant's record to show a course in educational psychology and another in teaching methods. Nor will it be overcome by subjecting the new "hire-ins" to the indignity of taking courses. Improvement is an in-service proposition in the nature of research wherein the instructor is urged to gather evidence on the progress of his students. This is a high-handed way of saying that continuous evaluation of student development is necessary and this evaluation must be as broad as the goals or objectives held for the instruction. Many instructors will need considerable assistance in learning to develop and use comprehensive evaluation procedures. The assistance may be made available either in the person of the administrator or through designated professional staff people.

The defining of instructional goals in terms of behavior, the selecting of learning experiences which promise to produce the changes desired, and the refining of evaluation procedures are three avenues to the selection and development of proper institutional activities. This formula applies not only to classroom enterprises but also to all behavior-changing enterprises in which the school may be engaged.

The first major responsibility of administration in the selection and development of institutional activities, then, is the progressive refinement of a point of view. This procedure is not simply arm-chair speculation and dialectics. It is an engaging, experimental undertaking. It involves gathering evidence and making evaluations of the evidence. For some college or university it may be the only research in which it engages. For *any* college or university it is the fundamental or underlying research which it should pursue.

Principles of Program Development

Any single college or university will need to circumscribe its own activities. In doing so it should bear in mind the unique contributions of other institutions serving the same geographical region or the country as a whole. A "balance sheet" should be maintained for all higher education so that certain services are not provided in superabundance while other activities are badly neglected.

Four principles are presented to serve as guides in defining the program.

Meeting Social Needs. Any line of endeavor is acceptable as a proper enterprise for higher education if it involves a persistent social need or problem to which formal education may offer a partial solution. This statement of principle recognizes that many social needs and problems will be met by schools operating below the maturity level of higher education.

Such a broad interpretation of the potential of higher education runs counter to the belief that only the "respectable" arts and sciences are worthy of consideration. It is enlightening to observe in this connection that all the arts as well as the sciences originated in practical situations. As Butts[12] has said:

. . . . When modern educators eulogize the universality and permanence of truth and knowledge, it is well to remember that organized knowledge grew up in connection with the social necessities of controlling the physical environment and human conduct. When they speak of the desirability of studying "pure" science apart from its

[12] *A Cultural History of Education,* by R. Freeman Butts (New York: McGraw-Hill Book Co., Inc., 1947, p. 18).

practical applications, it should be remembered that science appeared in the midst of a practical and social situation. . . .

Arithmetic as a means of counting and keeping accounts grew out of the commercial process of exchanging goods and out of the political need for levying and collecting taxes. Geometry was refined in the process of controlling the floods of the Nile and in constructing canals and buildings. Astronomy was related to navigation and to the development of the calendar. Medicine developed as a means of warding off or curing illness; art and music were a part of religious ceremonies.[13] Beyond these primitive beginnings the major part of the natural science groundwork was laid by individuals and societies operating outside the confines of the university, although a few free universities did contribute significantly. As the scientific method became a refined procedure for expanding and verifying knowledge, the university came to be the place where these findings were preserved and the frontiers expanded.

Simply stated, education has come to be a method for getting things done. For example, a positive relationship between higher education and the material standard of living has been claimed and verified. Research activities, especially in the areas of agriculture and manufacturing industry, are noteworthy examples. From the instructional standpoint the standards of medical, dental, and engineering practice have been raised since the basic preparation for these professions has been assigned to institutions of higher learning. So convincing is the evidence in this regard that there is now no forseeable limit to the range of arts and sciences which higher education may undertake to improve. The scope of the offering in higher education is as comprehensive, in theory at least, as the range of socially approved activities of society. This generalization applies not only to matters of instruction

[13] Ibid., pp. 18–19, *passim.*

but equally as well to the area of research and to the service activities of higher education.

Higher education should be creative in establishing its program. It should search continually for those problems which are pressing upon society and for minor ills which may become acute. The problem so located may be broad and general in scope such as developing international understandings; it may be a domestic problem such as inadequate housing; it may be a local problem such as a crop disease; it may be a problem of a labor group such as contract negotiation procedures. Higher education should select its activities not on the basis of "privileged learnings" for "privileged persons" but rather upon the contribution which education can make towards solving a problem of social consequence.

Since the number of these problems is too great for an institution to undertake it should make its choices on the basis of the degree of social consequence and in light of the institution's area of operation. The decisions so reached should be markedly different among institutions of the same type as well as among the several schools of higher education—the community college, the land-grant university, the area technical institute, the theological seminary, the teachers college. The procedure advocated is in contrast with imitating the program of a "recognized" institution, with continuing a routine offering simply because it is established, with accepting a classical notion of cultural learnings.

Serving a Greater Student Body. The activities of higher education should be sufficiently broad as to meet the needs of those persons desirous of attending and capable of benefitting from an education which can be devised for them. This principle is essentially a restatement of the first principle since "needs" are in large measure socially induced.

The President's Commission on Higher Education has concluded that 49 per cent of the people have the "mental ability to complete 14 years of schooling with a curriculum of general and vocational studies that should lead either to gainful employment or to further study at a more advanced level." [14] The Commission also estimates that 32 per cent of our population "has the mental ability to complete an advanced liberal or specialized professional education."[15]

In a general way we think of 15 to 20 per cent of the 18–21-year age bracket of our population being enrolled in some type of higher education. There are numerous reasons why colleges do not attract and hold a larger percentage of those eligible to attend, the cost factor being most frequently mentioned. However, there is reason to believe that the lack of student interest or motivation is equally as much a cause.

Havighurst[16] has reported on studies in several midwestern communities to this effect:

> . . . . on the basis of these studies it can be said that the motivation barrier is at least as important as the economic barrier in keeping these young people out of college. That is, fully as many able young people fail to go to college because they lack the desire as those who fail to go because they lack the money. . . .

An increase in percentage of persons attending higher education will extend at a much greater rate the heterogeneity of their interests and purposes. Different interests, occupational and otherwise, must be appealed to and a greater range of activities provided. Reflecting upon the secondary school growth and development it now seems ironical and the famous Committee of Ten (1893) was proclaiming the merits of substantially the same education for all high school pupils at the very time when the secondary school was on the thresh-

---

[14] President's Commission on Higher Education, *op. cit.*, p. 41.

[15] *Ibid.*, p. 41.

[16] "Social Implications of the Report of the President's Commission on Higher Education," by Robert J. Havighurst, in *School and Society* (67: 259, April 3, 1948).

old of its tremendous development. It is worth conjecturing whether the periodic clamor of a same-for-all "general education" at the higher education level is equally poorly timed.

Internal policies of the school may hinder the effective use of the instructional facilities which are available. One regulation that is greatly overemphasized is the "prerequisite" concept. A student may have good reason for choosing a course in "Public Finance and Taxation." In his effort to enroll he finds he must have passed "Principles of Economics II," which, in turn, has a prerequisite of "Principles of Economics I." This is a very simple sequence arrangement; others are much more complex and may become greatly involved by entering into another department where an additional series of requirements may prevail.

The arrangement is understandable in advanced and highly specialized fields. It is much less understandable where no proven relationship exists among the subject areas and where the sequence plan is used to control enrollment and to gain prestige by making courses appear as "advanced." Several assumptions are normally involved in addition to that of ability to pass the course. One is that the *instructor* or *department* has the purpose for offering the course and the purpose is to put something across. The student's purpose for taking the course is not considered valid unless he has proved his intentions by jumping the hurdles placed in the way. The net result of this regulation and others of a similarly restrictive nature is to prevent the formulation of a program for a student in light of his needs and interests. It also makes for a mass-production approach to education, and it yields a paradoxical situation of a student starving, educationally speaking, in the midst of plenty.

Off-campus groups should also be considered in determining institutional activities. Whatever may be said of the need for adult education has direct implications for higher education. As is generally known, the age distribution of the population in the United States continues to shift in favor of adults. In 1900, approximately 44 per cent of the population was nineteen years old or younger and 56 per cent twenty years old and older. By 1945 there were twice as many persons twenty years old and older than there were in the younger age group.

It is no longer possible for a person to obtain in his youth an education adequate for the full lifetime ahead. Nor can solutions to current problems be postponed until the coming generation matures. The implication is not that adults are constantly in need of a variety of college courses. Rather, the service to be rendered is largely that of helping adults to determine their own educational needs and in aiding them to meet these needs. The form which an educational plan takes may be greatly unlike college courses. There are instances, however, when regular college courses, tailored to fit the occasion, may meet the needs very acceptably.

The "social shortage" approach is applicable in determining the off-campus services. A given community may need assistance in making a survey of its education, recreation, and health facilities; the expressional arts may be badly neglected in a community or area and in need of outside stimulation; an occupational shift may require the retraining of technicians. A college of education may offer specialized professional services to teachers in advising about matters of reading or of speech correction, or by interpreting concepts of human growth and development. Similar services may be rendered by the college of education to lay groups as well. Each college should be expected to know the needs of the clientele which it serves.

Maintaining a Balanced Program. Collectively considered, institutions of higher learning should establish a fair balance in the emphasis given to the several fields of knowledge and activity. Lack of good proportion is most noticeable in the area of research wherein the preponderance of funds and personnel is used in the natural sciences including biology and medicine.

As a case in point the typical land-grant school is characterized by its extensive farms, large barns, greenhouses, laboratories, and numerous "ag" buildings. Full-time experts develop bigger and better apparatus to spray pea aphids, breed better bulls, determine the optimum number of square feet of chicken house per chicken, and develop rapid-maturing tomato plants. Money, facilities, and personnel are available to publicize the findings and to carry the information directly to farm people. The same university may have a college of education. In the latter college a full-time research person would be a rare phenomenon. Yet problems which involve human relationships and learning can be solved only by the same kind of intellectual activity—applied in the same diligent way—as are problems of crops, livestock, fuels, lubricants, and atomic energy.

It is, of course, relatively simple to appeal for funds before a state legislature or a board of overseers composed of businessmen, where the expenditure promises to produce tangible results in the way of bushels of wheat per acre or pounds of butterfat. And the importance of such research is very great. But the data supporting the need for research in the social sciences, broadly defined, must be marshalled with as much thoroughness as pertains to the natural sciences. One means toward this end is through the participation of faculty members representative of all departments in outlining research needs and in determining what facilities are required to carry on effective research in the several fields.

Two asides merit attention in the treatment of a balanced

research program. The first pertains to basic research. As the Steelman[17] report urged, there is considerable need in this country for basic research in contrast with developmental research and the university shares a major responsibility in this regard. Of basic research, the Report states:[18]

As a people, our strength has lain in practical application of scientific principles, rather than in original discoveries. In the past, our country has made less than its proportional contribution to the progress of basic science. Instead we have imported our theory from abroad and concentrated on its application to concrete and immediate problems. This was true even in the case of the atomic bomb.

A second aside pertains to a minimum research program. The least research that may be expected of any institution of higher learning is that it should be engaged continually in evaluating the results of its program, no matter how restricted the offering may be. The research may be confined to studies of graduates, drop-outs, effectiveness of instructional methods, and to other individual and community data presented in Chapter XI.

To proceed with the topic, maintaining a balanced program, the area of service activities may be considered. The service activities of higher education should vary from institution to institution, just as research activities differ. In fact, variation in research programs is cause for differences in service activities. For example, a university, strong in its basic industrial research, serves the manufacturing industries. A community college which makes careful studies of occupational opportunities in the area serves by rendering occupational information.

Higher education has tended to pattern the services which

[17] President's Scientific Research Board, *Science and Public Policy*, Vols. 1–5 (Washington, D. C.: U. S. Government Printing Office, 1947).
[18] *Ibid.*, Vol. 1, p. 4.

it renders. The most prevalent activities include extension classes chiefly of a self-supporting nature, the interpretation of the research conducted at the institution through agents and publications, and the maintenance of speaker and consultant bureaus. Numerous other services are rendered such as institutes and clinics for designated groups, package library facilities, community surveys, the operation of radio stations, and specific training for labor and management groups. But the widespread acceptance of the latter services has not prevailed.

Integrating the American Way of Life. Higher education should develop and pursue institutional activities which make for broad human sympathies and understandings rather than sponsor allegiances to selected social, economic, political, religious, and racial groups.

Bias and prejudice may be maintained either wittingly or unintentionally and much of this is done through the selection and development of institutional activities. Establishing hierarchies of curriculums and of departments is instrumental toward this end. Maintaining artificial dualisms such as cultural *versus* practical and general education *versus* vocational education is a contributory factor.

Much of the confused thinking which leads to incompatibility among individuals and groups stems from the belief that there is a single educational pattern which constitutes the "best" education. A person so educated is "cultured." A person not so educated is lacking culture.

But culture is indigenous to a social order. A concept of culture which does not grow out of the basic premises of the society leads to an education which is unsound for that society. America has rejected the plan of a leisure class and a toiling, sweating peasantry. American tradition holds in high regard all work that is socially useful. As a result the American concept of culture is at variance with traditional concepts which have been described in this manner by Dewey: [19]

> . . . . Traditionally, liberal culture has been linked to the notions of leisure, purely contemplative knowledge and a spiritual activity not involving active use of bodily organs. Culture has also tended, latterly, to be associated with a purely private refinement, a cultivation of certain states and attitudes of consciousness, separate from either social direction or service. It has been as escape from the former, and a solace for the necessity of the latter.

The writer believes that a person living in a democratic society is cultured to the extent that: (1) he is acquainted with the forces which influence the well-being of man; (2) he participates in controlling these forces for the common good; (3) he is able to make his way economically in a socially accepted manner; and, (4) he obtains from each experience an optimum of meaning and understanding.

Education which produces a cultured person in accordance with the above definition is *good* education. Labels of "general," "special," "vocational" simply becloud thinking.

A further obstacle to the operation of higher education as an integrative force in American life is the rigid earmarking of services to segments of the population. This condition prevails when the instruction is geared strictly to an élite group or where the point of view of the college coincides with the special interests of a pressure group. Or it may come about through the services purchased by an individual or a group.

Funds granted and controlled by legislative enactment may also be divisive. The Extension Service of the United States Department of Agriculture, working largely through state universities, has established a precedent of providing services to a specified group. Through this agency it is possible for rural and farm persons to be assisted, for example, in

[19] *Democracy and Education,* by John Dewey (New York: The Macmillan Co., 1916, p. 358).

problems of nutrition, home economics, and home management. But quite obviously families of industrial workers encounter these same problems as well as other problems peculiar to labor. Labor organizations are, therefore, currently seeking federal legislation and federal funds to provide a program of extension education for labor comparable in intent to that provided for rural and farm persons.

The fundamental issue involved is the group allegiance which is engendered by a series of special educations originating at the federal level. With two or more entries in the field, lobbies will be maintained to assure an uninterrupted flow of funds from the federal government. The tactics employed by these pressure groups will encourage group antagonisms. Furthermore, with the programs of education stereotyped by law, local needs are made to conform to the pattern. This results in offerings which are oblique to the true needs of a community.

The closely dovetailed social and economic order suggests the policy of offering educational services wherever they are needed and without the rigidity of legislative control. The administration of a program at the local level *by agreement* may be restricted to a homogeneous group. That is, an institute may be operated for union stewards and attendance confined to persons of this category. Or, an institute may be operated for management personnel with attendance restricted to management representatives. But since these arrangements are reached by agreement, and upon consideration of the circumstances involved, there would not be the heavy hand of outside control insisting that artificial separations be perpetuated.

The Outlook

The era of greatness for higher education in America lies in the present and in the future. Higher education has performed commendably in those areas where its objectives have been tangible and clear. It has performed less well where the purposes have been obscured by the blind following of traditional practices, or where its sensitivities have been dulled by the chanting of incantations which proclaim the universality of a segment of man's knowledge.

Higher education must refine, interpret, and perpetuate the American way of life. This it can do through helping persons to formulate a philosophy of life, through assisting people to develop their abilities to meet their personal and social problems, through advancing the frontiers of knowledge, and through extending educational opportunity to a continually expanding clientele.

CHAPTER XIV

EVALUATING SOME EFFORTS TO ACHIEVE DEMOCRACY IN ADMINISTRATION

EDWARD J. SPARLING

Roosevelt College of Chicago

JOHN DEWEY[1] pointed out that a desirable social group is one in which "there are many interests consciously communicated and shared," and in which
"there are varied and free points of contact with other modes
of association." If these are criteria of good social grouping,
and if an academic community is first of all a social group—
then it would seem to follow that democratic administration
should seek to achieve within the academic community an
interwoven, interpenetrative sharing of powers and accountability.

THE BASES FOR DEMOCRATIC ADMINISTRATION

At least three bases for organizing the school administration are apparently possible: isolation, consultation, and participation. The above frame of reference rejects isolation
which would separate completely the functions of administration, faculty, and students. Consultation, emphasizing the

---

[1] *Democracy and Education*, by John Dewey (New York: The Macmillan Company, 1928 edition, p. 97).

democratic idea of good communication, is being experimented with in a number of colleges and universities. Participation has been rarely tried, and then only on a limited scale. Consultation and participation would, however, be the only possible bases upon which to build a democratic administrative structure.

SOME METHODS NOW BEING TRIED

One of the most significant experiments in democratic administration was initiated in 1938 in the municipal colleges of the City of New York.[2] The college faculty, through its Council, a Committee on Budget and Personnel, and its privileges of electing department chairmen, was given broad consultative but not final powers. In 1948, ten years later, Ordway Tead[3] made a preliminary appraisal of this experiment. He reported the results as being "probably better and more satisfactory than we might have anticipated."[4] His critical remarks, however, seem to justify the following general inferences: Democratic sharing of powers and accountability results in onerous and time-consuming committee work. This expenditure of time is usually resented by many faculty members who therefore entertain the notion that more democracy in administration interferes with good teaching; second, faculties tend to seek powers but avoid accountability; third, provisions for widespread faculty participation in determining policy creates temptations for the faculty to exercise authority over policy *execution* instead of confining interests to policy *adoption*; fourth, if faculty members are permitted to elect department chairmen, some ill-advised selections will be made on the basis of "log-rolling" and "apple-

[2] See By-laws, New York City Board of Higher Education, Part II, Article XI.

[3] "Faculty-Administration Relationships in the College of New York: A Ten-Year Appraisal," by Ordway Tead, in *American Association of University of Professors Bulletin* (34:1::67–78, Spring, 1948).

[4] *Ibid.*, p. 70.

polishing," although this might occur no matter what method was used; fifth, when power on faculty appointments is delegated to department chairmen, there is danger that weak department heads will be reluctant to initiate action on strong applicants who might invite unfavorable comparison; sixth, provisions for formal consultation between faculty and trustee committees are not found to be very meaningful; finally, despite the difficulties, the New York experiment assures, in Tead's words,[5] "a fuller desirable measure of *advance* agreement between administration and faculty."

In a somewhat different approach, Antioch College has pioneered in trying to make its campus a laboratory of democracy. A key instrument is its Administrative Council made of seven faculty members and three students. This Council participates in the election of the president, advises the trustees in the determination of educational policy, consults with the president on the general management of the college and community, and elects every third person of a nineteen-man board of trustees.

Goddard College in Plainfield, Vermont, has sought an even fuller kind of democracy by giving a student Educational Policies Committee an influential voice in curricular matters. Furthermore, all teaching staff have equal rank, and the faculty assist in the nomination of the president, who serves for a fixed term of seven years.[6] As at Antioch College, there is at Goddard College an emphasis on *community*, not just *government*, with machinery set up to insure a participating voice by all who are governed. President Pitkin believes that the Goddard system provides for greater sharing

---

[5] *Ibid.*, pp. 71–72.

[6] The idea of fixed terms for deans, presidents, and department heads is often mentioned in the literature on education administration, but the idea is seldom tried and, so far as the writer knows, has never been evaluated or critically appraised. This idea is apparently worthy of further exploration.

of interests between students and faculty and has eliminated cleavage between faculty and administration.

Several institutions have made efforts to establish more direct relationships between faculty and trustees. The University of Wisconsin has a Regent-Faculty Conference Committee which is "empowered to make recommendations to the appropriate person, board, or agency on any matter relating to or concerning the university. . . ." [7] President Fred estimates that this committee is an excellent medium for exchanging ideas between the faculty and the regents. Wellesley College provides informal opportunities for faculty and trustees to work together in such common areas of interest as the Mayling Soong Foundation, the Pension and Insurance Board, Friends of the Library Committee, and Friends of the Art Museum. Former President Horton reports that all these functional groups are brought together at an annual dinner. The Wellesley faculty also elects one nonfaculty member to the Board. Mrs. Horton feels that this brings to the Board "the point of view of somebody who knows how professors feel about things," although she affirms that it is the duty of the President to "represent" the faculty at all meetings of the trustees. Cornell University has three members of the faculty, chosen by the faculty, who sit with the board and with the executive committee, but they do not have a vote.

Carnegie Institute of Technology has a provision for a faculty-trustee committee, but it has never been used. Commenting on this provision, President Doherty remarks: "I feel that this provision should be available in case of emergency, for example if the president should be intransigent, and thus is useful to faculty morale. But an administration would be in an unfortunate position if such a channel by-

[7] In this chapter quotations from the several presidents referred to are taken from the writer's correspondence with them.

passing the president were actively used. If there are mutual respect and a sincere desire to achieve a common purpose, such a channel, except as a safeguard, is both unnecessary and, I believe, undesirable; if such respect and desire do not exist, something is wrong that more machinery won't solve."

At California Institute of Technology the Board's by-laws permit faculty representation on its executive committee, but they are not on it because the faculty itself does not wish to be. The reason for this attitude, as stated by President DeBridge is "simply that it put the faculty in an awkward position being on a committee which in principle has authority over the president, while at the same time as faculty members they were responsible to the president."

In practically all colleges and universities there are provisions for some faculty self-government, limited in varying degrees by authority granted by the trustees. Authority most frequently delegated is, of course, in regard to purely academic matters such as curriculum organization and content. Even curriculum aims are much more firmly in faculty hands than they were a generation ago. Except at Black Mountain College, the author has found no delegation to the faculty of final control over personnel and budget matters in any of this country's institutions of higher learning.

Amherst College's "Committee of Six" is a good example of the kind of executive power exercised in the process of limited faculty self-government. This committee's powers upward to the president are consultative and advisory, but it has the somewhat unique privilege of reporting its recommendations on promotions and retirements directly to the trustees.

Efforts to effect better consultative relationships between faculty and administration are also rather widespread. A good example of this is at the Massachusetts Institute of Technology where a Staff-Administration Committee is made up of seven members of the faculty and seven members of the administration. One of the faculty members serves as chairman. This committee is for discussion purposes only, but out of the discussions have grown useful actions such as the adoption of a new tenure policy which both the corporation and the faculty accepted.

THE WAY TO PARTICIPATION

Because of the corporate nature of the American college and university, final powers always reside in some kind of a corporate board. Faculty members only rarely have a voice in determining membership on these boards. At first glance this does not appear to be alarming, especially if there is a clearly accepted assumption that institutions of higher learning are not different from business organizations. But if we reject this assumption, we must seek rather precisely to define what the faculty member is. Is he similar to a business employee, a stockholder in a corporation, a voting member of a political unit? Or is his status something different from all three?

A faculty member can hardly be classified merely as a professional employee, a stockholder, or a citizen of a special political entity. The college or university campus is a unique community and must empirically work out its own kind of administrative structure. The unique element in an academic community is that freedom to search for truths is an openended process. No kind of external control, in whatever degree, would seem congenial with the nature of this freedom. Ought we not then aim and work toward the ideal of a community of completely self-governing scholars? The way would seem to lie beyond consultation, somewhere in the area of more and more direct participation by faculty members in deciding the distribution of administrative powers, in providing checks on those powers, and shouldering the burdens of accountability.

Founded in 1945, Roosevelt College attempted to erect a more democratic administrative structure than is usually found in American colleges. In this chapter an attempt will be made to indicate the essential feature of this structure and to evaluate it briefly. The fact that this administrative structure is substantially unchanged after four years of operation is itself an achievement. Many other laudable results could be pointed out, such as an unusually low faculty turnover and the ability in a highly competitive market to build up rapidly a strong faculty because men and women were greatly attracted by more academic freedom. This is a preliminary evaluation of a so-called "administrator." Naturally any evaluation would depend somewhat upon the vantage point from which the view was taken. At this time the evaluation is preliminary and personal, although the opinions of some faculty colleagues were solicited.

The Board of Trustees at Roosevelt College is interracial and intercreedal. Members come from the fields of finance, business management, organized labor, journalism, law, teaching, the judiciary, government, and industry.

The presidency of the college and the deans' positions have a unique feature. All of them must submit to a triennial vote of confidence from the faculty, and in the case of the deans, their original appointments (though made by the trustees) must be confirmed by a two-thirds faculty vote. The purpose of the triennial confidence vote, as stated in the faculty constitution, "is to convey to the President, and through him to the Board, for its guidance, the sentiment of the College Faculty." No attempt has been made to define the size of the triennial vote necessary to mean "confidence" or "no confidence," but it should be pointed out that in the first triennial voting all of the deans sustained better than a two-thirds vote of confidence. Moreover, to date no trustee appointment has failed to be sustained by the faculty. It is too early to state whether or not this confidence vote is wise; it is safe to say that an overwhelming majority of our faculty, including the writer, believes it is. Certainly no other feature of this faculty government has attracted more interest.

Department chairmen are elected for three-year periods by a majority vote of the executive committee of the appropriate school council. The school dean, the dean of faculties, and the president are voting members of each school council.

A voting faculty member is any full-time appointee regardless of rank, and any part-time appointee with more than one year of service. Major administrative officers are also faculty members.

The important group bodies are:

    a. The Administrative Council, made up of the president, the deans, and the controller. The Council meets fortnightly.

    b. The Administrative Cabinet, made up of the president, the deans, and the controller and all major department heads such as the registrar, director of admissions, and director of health service. The function of the Cabinet is primarily consultative and it meets monthly.

    c. The Deans Conference, a liaison body of the deans, primarily for consultation and study. Actions are either recommendations or are within the power of the individual deans.

    d. The College Senate, made up of elected representatives of the departments, is the top governing body of the faculty. One senator is elected for every eight (or fraction thereof) voting faculty members of each department. The Senate's powers, though broad, are limited by the faculty constitution, any amendment to which must be approved by the trustees of the college. Trustee approval has been almost automatic to date. An unusual formula was worked out in the matter of sharing between the Senate and the entire faculty the right to pass constitutional amendments. If the Senate votes down an amendment which received 30 per cent of the Senate vote, or if an amendment is passed with less than a 70 per cent majority, the amendment must be referred to the whole faculty for a vote. The College Senate meets monthly.

e. The School Councils are elected for one year by the academic departments. Senators are members of the appropriate Council, and a department elects an additional representative to the Council for each Senator. For example, a department with twelve voting faculty members would have two Senators and two additional Council members, thus totaling four Council representatives.

The formulation and interpretation of administrative policy resides largely in the Administrative Council, although on crucial matters such as tenure and promotion policy the Administrative Council refers proposed changes to the College Senate. Any Senator may also introduce changes. On individual promotions and tenure cases the appropriate School Council's executive committee votes, usually after reviewing the recommendations of the department (obtained by secret ballot), the department chairman, and the school dean. These votes are advisory because the final decision is in the hands of the president.

Budget-making is the responsibility of the deans and the president, subject to final approval by the trustees. A faculty committee, however, meets frequently with the Administrative Council during all stages of budget planning.

The faculty shares with the trustees the privilege of making appointments to the Board. The Senate elects six faculty Board members (not necessarily Senators) to the twenty-six man Board.

The grievance procedure, a vitally important part of the faculty constitution, will be discussed below.

In addition to a traditional weekly calendar of events published by the dean of faculties for the faculty, staff, and the students, two other communication devices have proved helpful. The first is a monthly *Newsletter* written by the president. This is sort of a "State of the College" report, including frank discussions of the College finances and explanations of important decisions of administrative policy. The second device is a monthly faculty discussion organ called *Issues*. It is edited by a faculty committee appointed by the Senate and is published at college expense. This publication is the "Hyde Park Corner" of the academic community, and in it the debate waxes hot and heavy, usually centering around administrative policy, academic policy, and the pros and cons of proposed constitutional changes.

The following chart is an attempt to show the distribution of power and accountability in the administrative structure of the college:

Probably the three most important things to be said about the Roosevelt College structure are:

First, no attempt has been made to take final power out of the hands of a board of trustees. In this sense the experiment could never be a complete attempt at direct faculty participation and self-government. Roosevelt College was born out of a conflict over academic freedom and racial discrimination. The writer's experience with a previous board of bankers and lawyers compelled him to propose that this new college should have a board of which 51 per cent should be faculty members elected by the faculty. The faculty members themselves voted down this proposal because they did

ADMINISTRATIVE STRUCTURE OF ROOSEVELT COLLEGE

	Faculty appointments	Promotions	Tenure	Budget	Administrative policy	Appointment to Board	Grievance	Power to amend corporate by-laws	Power to amend faculty constitution	Curriculum aims and policies	Curriculum content	Curriculum organization	Student discipline, academic and non-academic
Board of Trustees				X		S	X	X	X				
President	X	X	X	C	XS		C						X
Controller				C									
Dean of Faculties	CV	CV	CV	C			C			C	C	C	
Dean of Students				C									CV
School Dean	CV	CV	CV	C			C			C	C	C	
Department Chairman	PCV	PCV	PCV							C	C	C	
Faculty Member	PCV	PCV	PCV			S			CS	C	C	C	
Administrative Council					S								
Administrative Cabinet					S								
Deans Conference					C								
College Senate							C		CS	X			
School Councils		PCV	PCV							C	X	X	
Faculty Committees				C	C								

X — Decision-making authority
P — Voting participation
C — Power of consultation and recommendation (formalized)
V — Strong veto influence on decision-making authority
S — Shared decision-making authority

not wish to shoulder such complete responsibility. However, a board was created which was so broadly representative of all segments of this community that no one point of view in our society could dominate. Twenty per cent of the board are faculty members elected by the faculty with full voting powers.

Second, an attempt was made to formalize consultation. Most consultative methods are informal, but by making them formal and obligatory the influence of faculty sentiment is greatly enhanced. Formalized consultation is an essential next step toward participation.

Third, three specific methods of direct participation are in practice: *One*, full participation in board membership by the faculty; *two*, submission of deans' appointments to two-thirds confirmation vote of faculty with subsequent triennial faculty votes of confidence for these deans and the president; *three*, election of department chairmen for three-year terms by elected representatives of the schools. All three of these "radical" innovations have worked reasonably well.

ELEMENTS OF APPRAISAL

Following are some of the more important things to be said about the organization described above:

Concerning the "representative" board of trustees, the following seems to be true: Individuals on the board have not "represented" Catholics, Jews, Protestants, or anything else. Individual board members have always acted with the total welfare of the college in mind. There have, for example, been no serious differences of opinion between business and labor members, and the board has never split on a faculty-public member basis. Furthermore, even though the board retains final authority, it has never used that authority to imperil academic freedom in any conceivable way. The role of faculty members to date has in some respects been a negative one. Their presence may have deterred certain actions unpopular to the teaching staff, but the faculty members have not attempted to influence public members on vital budget matters. This reflects a realization that the faculty members are not in a position to press for certain policies because of their inability to tap rich sources for contributions. The traditional pattern has been that trustees should be a majority of persons who are financially influential and capble of strengthening the financial position of the institution. Roosevelt College has not departed from this traditional pattern. The writer, however, questions this tradition and firmly believes in strong faculty representation not only on private institutional boards but especially on the boards of municipal and state institutions because it is essential that faculty sentiment be conveyed directly to political leaders and the public by means of trustee policies.

The task of the president and the deans is undoubtedly more time consuming and difficult than in a less democratic arrangement. In two specific instances the president's role is not clear: With some heat there is a current debate over the question of whether or not the president should "give his reasons" whenever his decision on personnel matters differs from the recommendation of a School Council executive committee. Second, in the grievance procedure, it is contended that the Senate's executive committee should review the decision of the president and report directly to the trustees instead of having the president report to the trustees after reviewing the decision of the executive committee. Finally, it should be reported that although most kinds of responsibility can be delegated, there is no way to delegate final responsibilities for the total welfare of the institution. The chief executive officer must always retain final responsibility and power commensurable with it. The crucial question is that both the powers and the responsibility be democratically derived and subject to checks by democratic processes.

When an attempt is made to delegate authority to elected groups and committees, it becomes crucially important that democratic methods of election and selection be employed. The most serious internal crisis at Roosevelt College has been over method. The controversy occurred over the question of the preferential ballot, i.e., proportional representation as a method of elections. After extended debate the faculty voted against proportional representation by a ratio of about seven to three. The sentiment for this method came almost solidly from the ranks of the social scientists, many of whom tend to equate proportional representation with democracy itself. In the opinion of the writer, proportional representation is not only *not* synonomous with democracy, it defeats democratic election processes because a determined minority is given a tool with which it can elect people who are pledged to place the objectives of a minority of the faculty above the total welfare of the institution.

The administrative procedure here described has not eliminated faculty differences and internal controversies. It may have lessened the intensity of opinion differences and kept these differences out in the open instead of allowing them to fester undetected, but so long as ultimate powers are retained by the administration, it is doubtful that complete freedom to differ without some fear of reprisal, and without some hardening of internal factional lines, can be achieved.

The majority of the faculty has shunned large measures of responsibility. This has most often taken the form of unwillingness to make unpleasant personal decisions. For example, there has been a lack of critical discrimination in some recommendations on promotions and tenure. Furthermore, when formalized powers of recommendation are in the hands of faculty executive committees there is a tendency to disrupt normal channeling because on matters of promotion, salary, and tenure some individuals tend to circumvent regular administrative channels and appeal cases directly to the committees. This kind of behavior allows a problem to get outside of channels before the normal administrative process has had a fair chance to solve it.

The grievance procedure is the necessary judicial machinery in a democratic academic community. Any full-time employee of Roosevelt College has a right to file a grievance whenever a serious difference of opinion involves a member of the faculty or the administrative staff. The grievance is originally heard before the administrative officer having jurisdiction. An appeal from his decision can be made in turn through the deans, the president, the executive committee of the Senate, and finally to the board. As referred to earlier, it is currently a matter of dispute whether the president or the Senate executive comittee should have the authority to refer a final grievance appeal to the board. This is important because in this instance the executive committee of the Senate could attain a status over the president. In the writer's opinion, this would not be desirable.

To date the grievance procedure has been criticized in five respects: First, it allows administrative action against a faculty member *prior* to a hearing before his peers. Second, this condition shifts the burden of proof from administration to individual, thus violating due process. Third, in one of the four cases heard to date, the advisory, judicial, and executive functions of individuals involved were not clear. In one instance, an advisory opinion was given by the executive committee of the faculty which at a later date sat in a judicial capacity. Fourth, there should probably be a "cooling off" period before grievance is initiated because this would allow chance for reconciliation and compromise, thus avoiding the expenditure of time, money, and emotional energy.

Fifth, there has not yet been ample experience to formulate clear-cut rules of procedure with respect to the admission of evidence. This lack of clarity has cluttered the record and prolonged considerably the hearings of grievances. These five points might well be noted by those who wish to construct a somewhat similar grievance procedure.

Finally, the case for board faculty participation in personnel decisions is based on the commendable premise that specialized knowledge of a teacher's competence by his own department colleagues and subject matter peers is of greatest importance in judging his work and in recommending promotions. It has been found, however, that in a few instances there is a tendency to sacrifice quality for the sake of friendships, peace, factions, and other irrelevant considerations. Furthermore, in rare instances individuals who cannot command majority support within their own department are apt to carry the case to a larger body (such as a School Council or its executive committee) whose decisions might be made on nonprofessional bases of close personal friendships or upon previously formed lines of internal factional alignment.

In the beginning of this chapter the reader was aware of John Dewey's principles applied to a democratic theory of administration. He has no doubt concluded that some of the things just said indicate that in practice the theory has not always worked out. He will then be justified in asking "why" —citing Dewey's contention that in his terms there can be no such thing as good theory and bad practice. If the practice has been bad, the theory must be changed. Is Roosevelt College ready, therefore, to scrap its theory of democratic self-government because some serious difficulties have been encountered?

The answer to this question can take two directions: First, the ends in view of the faculty participants in self-government may at a given time differ from the ends in view of administrators. These differences will occur under any system. In the system described above, it is indicated that at times there has been a lack of understanding and sharing. It is conceivable that faculty members of a given department might wish a chairman who will "simply leave them alone," not "push us around," whereas the dean may feel that a department is weak and needs strengthening. Certain unfortunate results might immediately be evident if any one view prevails, but in the long run and in the wider sense, the democratic theory will result in better administration. Presumably an experimental setting with freedom to differ and criticize will eventually bring those with "wrong" views to see the error of their ways. The way of intelligence is not to impose a "right" way; the way of intelligence is to keep inquiries running, to explore constantly and empirically the kind of practice being used. A second way to answer is to suggest that we reflect upon the processes being used. The proccesses, as we saw in the case of proportional representation, can work against rather than for democratic practice. But the writer's evaluation of proportional representation may be wrong too! Therefore, this chapter argues that a democratic theory of administration does demand that we safeguard the position to criticize our practices and that we have the freedom to improve them in the light of our experience. The kind of structure in operation at Roosevelt College helps greatly to make that freedom secure. Far from being discouraged with our results to date, the writer asserts that there are no ills in our democratic structure that cannot be cured by more democracy. Indeed the unparalleled development of the College could not have been achieved without widespread faculty participation throughout its four years of development.

There are, however, some important questions which the Roosevelt College experiment raises:

a. To what extent is democracy embedded in structure? And to what extent is it purely "spirit" or human motivation? For example, often when there has been difficulty in trying to interpret the faculty constitution some individual appeals to "the democratic spirit of our constitution."

b. What is the nature of a hierarchy of power? Can ultimate power be derived from "facts," and from the correlation of lower-level powers, or must ultimate authority be imposed by definition?

c. What is the proper role of compromise and consensus in administration? Are these merely devices which seek solutions on the level of the lower common denominator of agreement? Or are consensus and compromise really useful products of consultation and participation? At one extreme there may be a "packed" committee or governmental body which has no trouble reaching agreement; at the other extreme, agreement is often reached at such a low level of principle that consensus is merely verbal agreement or no agreement at all. The group process techniques of reaching agreement on which meaningful action can be based appear to be fertile fields for study by students of administration.

The following are cited as the most important achievements in faculty self-government at Roosevelt College: The faculty has worked out admirable criteria for promotions and tenure; the nature of the departmental chairmanship has been helpfully defined; the power to initiate action on promotion has not been concentrated in one or two persons but has been shared widely; a committee system has been evolved which distributes committee load and which wisely separates action responsibility from advisory responsibility; and finally, to a large degree there has been achieved in the school a healthy atmosphere of freedom, equality of opportunity, a sense of belonging, and a sharing of purpose and problems which has developed enthusiasm for democracy despite the pitfalls caused by the fallibility of individuals. Indeed, the greatest glory and the deepest purpose of democracy at Roosevelt College have been to set the stage for the free flow of ideas and open opportunity for individual development, and to protect these free flowing processes from those who would curtail them.

SUMMARY AND CONCLUSIONS

THERE are almost two thousand institutions of higher education in the United States, ranging from great universities enrolling many thousands of students, sometimes on a series of campuses, to small community colleges with a hundred or even fewer students each.

These institutions are all administered with a certain desire to serve American democracy. Their concepts of the best ways to carry out this aim are almost as varied as their numbers and their programs of instruction. Their administrative officers practice democracy in varying degrees. All of them presumably take into account the educational needs and desires of their communities, their students, and their faculties. They arrive, however, at surprisingly different outcomes in administrative theory and practice.

The present book has attempted to discuss and assess some main features of this diversity in theory and practice as related to the purposes and instruments of democracy.

SUMMARY

In Part One of this book, the role of higher education in the United States is described as related to the purposes of democracy, the principles of democratic association, the nature and functions of democratic administration, and the specific tasks of college and university administration.

The first chapter presents the thesis that a democracy is a manner of association whereby men order their own ways for their own benefit, and democratic education is the instrument whereby they change their own ways in the direction of their own ideals. Abilities to be cultivated or areas of knowledge to be mastered in higher education can therefore be determined only by direct approach to the people being served by the college or university. The first task of higher educational administration consequently is study of the institution's people, observation and evaluation of their activities and needs, and informing them concerning the implications and outcomes of the higher education they want.

The modern American university or college often evades this task. It seeks refuge in concentration on peripheral matters, deriving its purposes from studying its own procedures and basking in the light of its own adulation. Its great strengths for the task are its formal relationship to its people through a lay board and its specialization of administrators. Its most dangerous weakness is the separation of college teachers and students from administration.

Chapter II discusses the social responsibilities of higher education in a democracy. The labor movement, housing problems, health needs, community organization, and concentrations of economic power are cited as examples of areas in which higher educational institutions have great responsibilities for the furtherance of democratic ends.

The point is stressed that higher education, like education in general, has great potential strengths for carrying out the social changes a democracy needs to make, and that the college must help its students to understand these sources of power and to use them wisely for democratic ends.

The third chapter analyzes the task of college administration with particular reference to its supporting public. Here is described the rise of the new Presidential Man, an expert in money-raising, business management, and financial policy-making, who is not only excused from meeting the usual faculty standards of scholarship and academic experience but is often also regarded as being all the better choice because his prior administrative experience has been uncontaminated by educational service.

A president of this kind must make educational decisions like any other college administrator. He can get advice from his associates in business, politics, or finance. He can ask the faculty for advice and cancel plus and minus recommendations until he arrives at a "quantitative" answer. He can use his own intuition and "knowledge of men." But he cannot make daring appointments or display vital educational leadership.

In the college of liberal arts, the chief task of the president is to help release the talents of the faculty and students. This requires great energy to keep himself acquainted with the activities and ideas of the faculty and students, to help inform the trustees and the public concerning the college and the college concerning the community, and in general to act as chairman of a committee of the whole.

The fourth chapter defines the task of democratic administration as one of creating human relationships to free the human personality. The principle of free intelligence in these relationships assures every man that his contribution to group thinking counts and will be respected. The principle of participation keeps each individual in contact with the group. The principle of individuality utilizes idiosyncrasies of all group members. The principle of cooperation requires the experience of the joint task to give meaning and substance to individual efforts.

To deny any of these principles is to reduce markedly the effectiveness of any administration aspiring to be democratic. To apply them successfully in higher education, as in other areas of human enterprise, is to discover new sources of strength for the colleges and universities.

Chapter V pursues the problem of democratic association

further. The starting point in a search for higher levels of group aggreement is the belief that human personality has dignity and worth in itself. The test of any proposed action should be whether it will foster the richest possible living for all who will be affected by it.

To judge how effectively an institution is practicing democracy in its group activities, the following tests are proposed:

1. To what extent are the concerns of the group shared by its members?

2. To what extent is leadership shared by various members of the group?

3. Is the solution of the group accepted even though the status leader does not regard it as the "best" solution?

4. Is there mutual respect among the members, and are differences utilized to develop richer and deeper insights into the problem?

5. Is the group process used to release the creative potentialities of the members?

6. Does the status leader facilitate the process of reaching decisions on common problems?

In Part Two, certain administrative practices and organizations are examined. Chapter VI discusses various ways of determining institutional objectives. Among the agencies and groups that participate in this process are legislatures granting charters and (for public institutions) appropriating funds, courts which interpret legal and constitutional provisions for higher education, boards of regents or trustees which make regulations of their own that have statutory force.

In descending order of usual weight in making recommendations of policies to the legally constituted authorities are the president, the academic staff, the alumni, the students, and the nonacademic staff. In some institutions none of these, even the president, is seriously consulted on certain matters of great policy moment. In most institutions, some of these groups, e.g., the students or the nonacademic staff, are rarely consulted.

The unhealthy educational effects of denying opportunity to take part in policy-making are enumerated for various groups.

The influences on policy-making of other groups of various kinds, as for example, the great foundations, industrial concerns, government agencies, professional organizations, tax-savers associations, educational commissions, and the national and regional associations in higher education, are assessed critically.

The seventh chapter turns to the examination of a specific professional task, the determination of instructional activities, as an example of current ways of attempting to carry out the principles of democratic education in a college or university program.

The actual instructional procedures must be democratically based. That is, they must be understood, accepted, and operated by the faculty and the students to attain a level of reasonable quality. At this point precisely, a lack of sound democratic procedure is fatal to the success of the instructional program.

The steps by which those who must put instructional objectives into action are detailed with respect to the public to be served, the university and college administrations, and the faculty committees in divisions and departments. Attention is also given to ways in which the preparation of college teachers, their assignment to courses, and their classroom performance are related to the democratic development and operation of a good instructional program.

Chapter VIII looks at practices in faculty organization for democratic effectiveness, particularly in eight institutions of higher education, large and small, public and private, which were studied intensively. These practices range all the way from giving the president all administrative responsibility, without accountability even to a board of trustees, to cases in which detailed constitutions and by-laws provided extensive faculty participation in the affairs of the whole institution, faculty control of individual colleges, and student membership on certain boards and committees.

On the least favorable side were practices of granting power to deans solely at the pleasure of the president, of having deans delegate functions to faculty members and take the functions away at will, of having no faculty meetings, and of giving students no opportunity to take part in or even observe discussions of university affairs.

Of a more democratic character were such practices as legislative bodies of the whole faculty, elected councils and committees, participation in policy-making, budget planning, promotions, and appointments, and extensive opportunities for students to learn educational democratic procedures by having a share in them.

The ninth chapter deals with the composition of governing boards. The typical members of such boards are reported as members of the proprietary or conservative professional classes, and various proposals are reviewed for securing a more adequate representation of other sections of the public.

The chapter recommends that boards should be broadly representative of all the people and should include special representatives of the faculty. The possible difficulties of the latter proposal are reviewed and are judged to be far outweighed by the advantages to be gained from closer cooperation between the two main agencies who in practice must make policies for the American college and university, regardless of what the statutes and regulations say. The problem is so to organize the board in its relations to the public and the faculty that the policy-making job is done as well as possible.

Part Three examines the responsibility of administration in specific institutional tasks. Chapter X analyzes the process of selecting and appraising personnel. Four sets of criteria for judging high competence of university staff members were developed:

1. The statements and achievements of certain famous university leaders, as Charles William Eliot, Andrew Dickson White, and William Rainey Harper, were studied in an attempt to discover the characteristics of great administrators and teachers.

2. Professors of American history since 1875, who were so designated by contemporary teachers of history, were similarly studied.

3. The training of professors in outstanding schools of education was analyzed.

4. The conclusions of S.S. Visher in his study of scientists were also used.

The chapter concludes that a great university is an integrated whole in which president, deans, professors, and students are so placed that their individual capacities can be exercised in the fullest freedom for the most significant group results. This integrative principle is supported by the clustering around particular institutions and in particular decades of starred scientists and distinguished professors of history.

The chapter calls attention to the danger of interpreting democracy as a set of techniques rather than as a set of goals. It suggests faculty participation in the selection and appraisal of personnel, for example, only when the faculty becomes sufficiently educated to contribute adequately to this difficult task.

Chapter XI, dealing with receiving and distributing financial support, notes first that higher education today has three outstanding financial manifestations:

1. The sheer size in present numbers and the expansion to come.
2. The sources of financial support.
3. The distribution of funds.

For the financial support of higher education in 1965, on a six- or seven-billion-dollar scale, the chapter recommends that student fees should be drastically lowered, that government and private grants should be given to many students, that private philanthropy should be continued under proper conditions of institutional control of its own program, and most of all that there should be an increase in tax funds.

In distributing funds among higher educational institutions, a first problem is the extent to which private colleges should receive financial support from public sources. It is concluded that tax funds should be given only to publicly controlled institutions, whether by direct payments or by grants-in-aid to students.

The distribution of federal funds among the states should be so made as to help equalize educational opportunity.

Chapter XII discusses the higher educational institution's task of studying the students and their communities. Recognizing that the first goal of education for democracy is the proper development of the individual citizen and that such development can be achieved in a democracy only by a school continuously aware of the society of which the individual is and will be a part, these two interrelated responsibilities are discussed as they affect higher educational administration.

Of students an institution needs to know, appraise, and provide for physical health, emotional stability, intellectual traits, communication skills, tests of special skills in particular areas, occupational interests and capacities, social skills, democratic activities, values, and attitudes, subject-matter tests, and opinions of the instruction given the student.

Of the communities the college serves, it must know and appraise the vocational needs, physical security, health, natural resources, child-welfare and child-rearing patterns, artistic and recreational needs, social beliefs and aspirations, and governmental organizations.

Chapter XIII reviews the administration's responsibility in developing its program of teaching, research, and service activities. Every time a new department or a new course is added, the institution's area of operation needs to be redefined in some measure. Whenever an educational issue is discussed in relation to the job of the college, the nature of that job must be reexamined.

Rejecting such criteria as ability-to-handle-abstractions or pursuit-of-first-and-ultimate-truths, the chapter recommends the formulation of objectives in terms of behavioral change and the selection of experiences to produce the desired changes. Thus the fundamental research for any college or university is that of studying the learners and the processes by which their ways may be changed.

The program of learning activities should meet social needs both on and off the campus, should maintain a balanced offering among its various groups of persons to be served, and should prepare all its learners for intelligent membership in American society.

The final chapter evaluates certain efforts to achieve democracy in administration. Of three bases for organizing administration—isolation, consultation, and participation—it rejects the first, as not meeting the test of democratic association, and discusses consultation and participation as the only possible bases for a democratic administrative structure. Various methods of developing such a structure are illustrated by description of cases. These range from places where provision is made for a consultative committee or two on specific matters, to Roosevelt College of Chicago where the most complete attempt is being made at participation in administrative functions by faculty, students, and public.

The Roosevelt board of trustees is interracial and intercreedal and has members representing various community groups, including the faculty. The president and the deans submit to a triennial vote of confidence. No attempt has been made to take final power out of the hands of the trustees, but an attempt has been made to formalize consultation and to secure direct participation.

Conclusions

Confronted with the challenge of analyzing the nature and future direction of higher education in this country, university and college administrators and teachers have tended to react in one or the other of two chief ways. One small set of them, frightened with the immensity of the task of bringing reasoned order out of monstrous chaos, have fled to the shelter of the spiritual ideals of their sixteenth-century forebears. Their solution is to seek the ancient refuge of the search for eternal truth. A few of these unhappy souls have remained within the walls of the big universities, burrowing themselves in libraries and laboratories, pursuing a rarified search for truth in the environs of bigness and earthy activity. Still others have fled to little sanctums protected by indulgent millionaires. There they mumble over their sacred books, hoping by their academic bead-telling to bring back the halcyon days when masters could do no wrong. But millionaires today are not as indulgent as were some popes of old, and student disciples emerging from an education not suited to present-day needs become critical of that education.

The other and happily larger group of educators analyzing

the twentieth-century institution look to no simple solution for a direction of their efforts. There is the hard task of discovering a reasonable philosophy by which to reconcile industrialism to democracy, and themselves to their society. To this group the authors of this book hope to belong.

Thus the present authors see no evil in bigness as such, assuming, of course, that there is no impairment in the quality of the education thus provided. As is pointed out in Chapter XI, they expect their institutions to grow bigger, and a central task is to discover ways of financing this bigness. The authors do not hark back to the happy days of the élite student of the higher learning. They are willing to open the doors to all who will come—and more. They only ask that there be adequate study of those students and of the communities from which they come.

Unlike their colleagues in the ivory towers, they ask for no sheltering cloak, but are firm in the belief that their institutions should be tied to and dependent on their communities through boards responsible to the people. They ask, indeed, that these boards put even greater burdens on their institutions for proving their value by becoming more representative of the whole people and of the persons who belong to the college community itself.

The acceptance by the authors of these characteristics of institutions of higher education is premised on establishing a pragmatic philosophy which shall take into account all elements of the society in which American colleges and universities develop. Although perhaps not all of the authors of this book would agree *in toto*, the philosophy implies that what industrialism and competitive capitalism have done for this country has been in direct proportion to the amount of democracy the society has afforded itself. If industrialism is to yield even richer blessings, there will have to be a correspondingly sharp expansion of democracy, in which process institutions of higher learning must lead the way. As thus conceived, democracy is not antithetical to industrialism but is the motivating power and must become the directing force.

Thus democracy still takes as its credo "all men are created equal"—equal that is, in the opportunities given all men to develop their full powers, and equal in their rights to protect and direct those powers. For democracy is founded on a deep belief in the uniqueness and worth of every human being. It puts a burden on every human being to guard jealously that uniqueness in every other human being. It demands the development of a moral responsibility in each youth to use that uniqueness for the good of his society.

Accepting the responsibility of higher education for leadership in implementing the democratic *credo*, the authors have inquired into the *whats*, *whys*, and *hows*. They have begun with the watchwords of *fairness* and *effectiveness* in the institution which they fully expect may become the next level of universal education to which the nation may aspire. They have made their recommendations in terms of such principles as *free intelligence* and *cooperation*. When they have talked of machinery, they have described it as being of importance only if it be closely related to principles of operation. For the authors believe that the quality of human relationships developed in the college community, as in the world community, is more important than the mechanics of the process.

The authors have constantly reiterated the necessity for consistency in word and deed. The college community cannot exercise leadership in a democracy if the community itself is autocratic in its effects on students, faculty, or the lay public. There must be freedom for the student, the faculty member, and the administrator in finding new and better ways to pursue truth and to implement that truth in practice. As thus conceived, freedom means not lack of restraint or *laissez-faire*, but rather the opportunity to become a participant in a wide variety of learning situations.

To guide the unfolding and directing of free intelligence, colleges must have at their helms big administrators, those with great educational ideals and a deep feeling for the proper implementation of those ideals.

If the reader accepts the premises of the authors, he also accepts the principle of a secular institution based on religious and moral principles. In the last part of the nineteenth century, the fight to establish universities as opposed to colleges involved freeing some of the colleges and most of the state universities from the strictures of particularist doctrines and dogmatic theologies. Although most of the great presidents were deeply religious men, they saw this fight as involving the establishment of secular institutions. The institutions so conceived, however, were not relieved of moral responsibilities to the society in which they flourished.

The authors of this book believe in the tradition of the great presidents whose insistence on the moral anchor of the integrity and worth of the individual and the responsibility of the individual to his society has aligned them with those who would call man's highest aspirations his spiritual values. Their motto for the secular institution, in the words of Confucius, might well be, "On this Earth all men are brothers." They believe higher education should be administered in this spirit, with all the letters available to make that spirit live.

INDEX